SCHOLASTIC

Reading Response
That Really Matters to Middle Schoolers

LARRY LEWIN

New York ❖ Toronto ❖ London ❖ Auckland ❖ Sydney
Mexico City ❖ New Delhi ❖ Hong Kong ❖ Buenos Aires

Teaching *Resources*

Dedicated to Lucie, my new granddaughter, and to her brother, Colin; her parents, Donald and Frédérique; and her Nana

Grateful acknowledgement to the following teachers and their students for work included in this book:

Mark McKelvey, Millicoma Intermediate School, Coos Bay, Oregon

Julie Warner, Marietta High School, Marietta, Georgia

Christine Gonzalez, East Montana Middle School, El Paso, Texas

Eliza Sher, Sheldon High School, Eugene, Oregon

Diane Mattison, Springfield Middle School, Springfield, Oregon

Tom Cantwell, Cal Young Middle School, Eugene, Oregon

Theresa Alexander and Susan Aldrich, Calvary Christian Academy, Philadelphia

Craig Smith, New Hope-Solebury Middle School, New Hope, Pennsylvania

Heather Scheiber, Wantagh High School, Wantagh, New York

Dave Smith and Laura Scruggs, Briggs Middle School, Springfield, Oregon

Jud Landis, Sheldon High School, Eugene, Oregon

Allyne Lawson, Chatsworth High School, Chatsworth, California

Kevin Callahan, Madison Middle School, Eugene, Oregon

Julie Janecka, Lynn Middle School, Las Cruces, New Mexico

Mary Mendivil, Cesar Chavez High School, Delano, California

John Waldron, Paul W. Kutz School, Doylestown, Pennsylvania

Thank you also to my designer, Kelli Thompson, and my editor, Sarah Longhi.

Credits:

Pages 24–25 and 83: adaptations from *Paving the Way in Reading and Writing: Strategies and Activities to Support Struggling Students in Grades 6–12* © by Larry Lewin (2003). Reprinted by permission of Jossey-Bass; page 57: Levels of Thinking chart from *Learning to Teach* © 2005 by Linda Shalaway. Reprinted by permission of Scholastic Inc.; page 75: The Sentence Opening Sheet © by The Stack the Deck Writing Program, Tinley Park, Illinois. Reprinted by permission; page 99: Permission to print Webshot granted by Jean Craighead George; backcover: photograph © Lori Lohman.

Cover design by Maria Lilja
Interior design by Kelli Thompson

ISBN-13 978-0-439-79604-0
ISBN-10 0-439-79604-0

Copyright © 2006 by Larry Lewin.
All rights reserved. Published by Scholastic Inc.
Printed in the U.S.A.

2 3 4 5 6 7 8 9 10   31   14 13 12 11 10 09 08 07 06

Contents

FOREWORD

Hold the lesson plans and get out the highlighter: Larry's at it again, and we're the lucky recipients of his fertile mind. *Reading Response That Really Matters to Middle Schoolers* is not only a compelling argument for interactive literacy, it's a valentine to adherents of Habits of Mind and developmentally appropriate learning for young adolescents. Even better, Larry shows us how to implement these ideas in practical and measurable ways.

In this new book, Larry builds on the common sense and inspired pedagogy found in his previous books on reading, writing, assessment, and the Internet. His writing is personable and exciting, and his enthusiasm is genuine, even after 30 years of teaching. I can already hear the number one readers' response to this book: "I can't wait to try this with my students!"

Reading Response That Really Matters to Middle Schoolers takes teachers and students beyond the conventional "Answer the questions at the end of the chapter," "Describe the character most like you," or "Draw a picture of a pivotal moment in the story" activities commonly found in many classrooms. From the ChecBrics and innovative student-to-author memos and postcards to the clever ideas on how to get authors to actually respond to students, the strategies in this book live up to the promise of Louise Rosenblatt's transactional reading approaches. Students find meaning in the fiction and nonfiction texts they read, and, given the ample evidence in the book, transformation. Larry explains how to provide real audiences for students and how to get them writing for real purposes.

Above all, Larry emphasizes the process of thinking and writing. He shows us how to lead our students through the steps, while making instruction-assessments along the way. Formative assessment is a visible presence throughout the book, and Larry provides specific ideas for frequent checkpoints that provide feedback to students and guide our instruction. Like Barry Lane, Vicki Spandel, and Laura Robb, Larry shows us how revision will lead students to great writing and thinking.

That revision process teaches students that once something is written, it is not set in stone. To Larry, critical reading and writing are ongoing compositions, not superficial fly-by's on the way to state exams.

Teachers will appreciate Larry's practical approach. He provides plentiful authentic student samples of his ideas in action, plus reality checks for what to do when a lesson does not work exactly as planned. He also includes ideas for how to differentiate instruction and assessment for students at varying levels of readiness or who use different styles of learning. He models his own strategies, freely sharing specific formats that teachers are invited to use with students. His teaching-on-the-frontlines savvy is evident in every chapter. He makes sure we know how to manage all the details of teaching reading response by providing practical advice—readers will find tips on how to contact authors, and even what to do with letters to an author if the author is no longer living. Larry's ideas are based on classroom realities, and they are described intimately, with a candor not frequently shared by practitioners.

Larry clearly has a knack for dealing with the unique nature of middle schoolers and for teaching them. He shows us how to appeal to their desire to contribute, connect, and, yes, confront. His strategies guide young adolescents as they constructively critique published writings, including previously unassailable textbooks, and learn how to write successfully for different audiences and purposes. He helps students move beyond their own egocentrism, even providing strategies for instilling the inclination and tools for civil discourse—a refreshing component of already insightful ideas.

Anyone who visits the professional libraries of individual schools or teachers in the next decade will find wrinkled, dog-eared, and written-upon copies of *Reading Responses That Really Matter to Middle Schoolers*; it will be that well-used. It deserves an honored and accessible place on any language arts or English teacher's bookshelf. I look forward to the writing and thinking created by students whose teachers have read and implemented these practices.

—RICK WORMELI

Disney's American Teacher Award, Outstanding English Teacher of the Nation, 1996

Author of *Fair Isn't Always Equal, Summarization in Any Subject, Meet Me in the Middle*, and *Day One and Beyond*

TALKING BACK: STUDENT-WRITTEN CRITIQUES OF THE AUTHORS WE ASSIGN THEM

Sixth-grade teacher Mark McKelvey gave his students a new, never-before-used assignment: "Write a feedback memo to the author of the short story you just read," he told them, "to give that author your opinion of the story."

Shocking? Maybe not that strong, but surely surprising. Think about it: How often are your students invited to "talk back" to an author? How common is it for students to write a critique of published work they have been assigned to read in school and send it to the author?

Many elementary students have been given the opportunity to write a letter to a favorite author, but not as a critique. Students typically write fan mail to the authors to thank them for a great book, to ask about their lives as writers, what pets they have, or to inquire about the timeline for a next book. I imagine J. K. Rowling has received a few of these.

But I'll bet she has not received postcards, memos, or letters from young readers who not only tell her what they loved about her books but also what they didn't like; what caused them confusion; actions of a character that seemed incongruous with the character's personality; scenes that she could have expanded, deleted, or completely changed; or suggested plot lines for a new book.

Students are not asked to critique published authors. But they should be: A critique is a powerful way to motivate student writing, to motivate careful reading, and to force them to think critically.

Responding to an author taps into a natural instinct many students possess: the desire to *talk back to authority*. But when I say they like to "talk back," I am not encouraging rude, inappropriate, or sarcastic behavior. Rather, I mean that students like to speak up, be heard, and be taken seriously.

The talking-back instinct certainly was apparent in Mark McKelvey's sixth-grade class at Millicoma Intermediate School, in Coos Bay, Oregon. Check out his student Carissa's memo to author Leon LeWine who wrote the short story "Sidd's Excellent Adventure," about a couple who take their cat to the vet. (You may recognize it from the cover.)

To: Leon LeWine
From: Carissa
Date: 4/3/05
RE: "Sidd's Excellent Adventure"

Your story was all right. The main reason I didn't like it was because I don't like farces. The one thing I can visualize is the bright orange goo on the cat because I watch a TV show called C.S.I. and it does a lot of stuff like that. It was extremely easy to predict he was going to do something with orange goo, but what he did with it was funny. The part I didn't like with orange goo was when he was going to kiss Inga because that doesn't really appeal to this audience's age. I didn't really understand why you put what Sidd's tail looks like (para. 14, lines 6–7). And why did you worry what your face looked like (para. 14, line 7) when you can't see it when the black light is not on? How do cats wear glasses? I thought the cat with the glasses was a bit too tacky.

Can we hear this student's writing voice? Can we appreciate her literary analysis? Can we feel her desire to communicate her opinions to the author? Yes. Her writing comes through loud and clear.

Plus, she is revealing many aspects of her reading. First, she employs the literary term *farce*, which no doubt came up in class discussions about the story. She relates an element in the story to a television show, which reflects the useful reading strategy known as making a connection from the text to another source. She compliments the author on helping her visualize a scene and to make a prediction—other key reading strategies. She compliments the author on his use of humor. She comments on the inappropriateness for a scene for a sixth-grade "audience." And finally, she asks the author several questions about his decision to include certain details. She even cites the paragraph and lines to him.

And her tone of voice is not rude or obnoxious. It is polite, friendly, and sincere but also honest.

The Reader-Writer Circle Is Broken

What does it take for our students to *want to write* like Carissa did? Some of them do want to write, of course; some even love to write. But as they make their way through the grades, many of them lose their energy for writing. And despite our best efforts, too many students learn to view writing as a school assignment, a teacher mandate, or even a punishment. Too many students in grades 5 through 9 fail to realize that writing is for communicating. Real writers write to real readers for a variety of communication purposes: to explain something, to entertain, to share an experience, or to argue a point.

The typical school writing assignment masks the purpose of communication by instructing students to write *to* the teacher and *for* the teacher. This works wonderfully in the primary grades because kindergartners and first and second graders love to write to and for their dear teachers. It's new, it's fun, and it's so grown-up. But as the years pass, students tire of the same ol', same ol'. Write a report, write a personal narrative with strong characterization, write an essay. While these structures have solid instructional value, we need to break the mold if we want to resuscitate writing ability in our schools.

The National Assessment of Education Progress (NAEP) writing test data from 2002 reveals a good news/bad news report. The good news is that all tested grades (4, 8, and 12) showed an increase at the proficient level (represents a solid academic performance) from the 1998 test. The percentages of student proficiency show we are headed in the right direction:

Grade 4   22% to 26%
Grade 8   25% to 29%
Grade 12   21% to 22%

However, and this, I think, is a big "however," the above percentages mean that only about one-quarter of our students are proficient in writing. Two percent scored at an advanced proficiency—up from 1 percent in 1998. That means that about 73 percent are at basic (denoting partial mastery of knowledge and skills) or below basic levels of performance.

Also, in 2002, the College Board established a study titled "The Neglected R," prepared by the National Commission on Writing in America's Schools and Colleges. The Commission reports to Congress in an attempt to improve the quality of writing in the U.S. In its Executive Summary the Commission states:

> Writing is how students connect the dots in their knowledge. Although many models of effective ways to teach writing exist, both the teaching and practice of writing are increasingly shortchanged throughout the school and college years. Writing, always

time-consuming for student and teacher, is today hard-pressed in the American classroom. Of the three "Rs," writing is clearly the most neglected.

The Commission goes on to make a series of recommendations for initiating a "Writing Revolution."

Because this book will advocate writing about *reading*, let's look at the NAEP reading assessment, which measures student reading for a literary experience, reading for information, and reading to perform a task. The data is discouraging. Here's a comparison of the "at or above proficient" readers from 2002 to 2003 to 2005:

Grade 4   31% to 31% to 31%
Grade 8   33% to 32% to 31%

This means nearly 70 percent of our students are not proficient readers. Not good enough. Not nearly good enough.

ENCOURAGING STUDENTS TO TALK BACK

I will advocate in this book that teachers must rethink traditional writing and reading assignments that are not inspiring all our students to read and write. While I have nothing against the traditional book reports, five-paragraph essays, and research papers, I have experienced a far more motivated response from students when they are asked to "talk back" to authors.

Let's face it: Writing requires immense energy. To transcribe words onto paper, so much needs to happen. The ideas, information, opinions, and stories that reside inside the writer's head must travel from the brain, down the neck, across the shoulders, down the arm, through the fingers, out onto the paper. This requires energy, concentration, focus, stamina, and desire because while the thoughts are hatching, the writer also has to consider the exact words to select to express those thoughts, in what order to place them, what verb tense to use, how much detail to include, what punctuation to add, whether or not to be funny, direct, or subtle—all this, and much, much more. No wonder Hemingway is reported to have said, "I write with my blood."

Writing is all about having a true purpose and a real audience. Without either, writing becomes artificial, uninspired, flat, dead. Like too many of our students' papers.

The same is true for reading. How many of our students have developed a love of reading? All of them? Most of them? Some of them? Or not enough of them? If your experience answers "not enough of them," then we had better ask the question, "Why not?"

I believe it is because reading can be difficult. And I am fairly good at it with 50 years of reading experience under my belt. Reading is difficult because it requires a transfer of ideas from the mind of an author to the mind of the reader. The author, a person who believes that his or her experiences, ideas, opinions, and observations are worthy of sharing, writes these thoughts onto paper (or types onto a computer) to share with a wider audience. The medium for these important thoughts is, of course, printed words. The words serve as the *middleperson*, the conduit, from the author to the audience, from the writer to the reader, as this diagram shows.

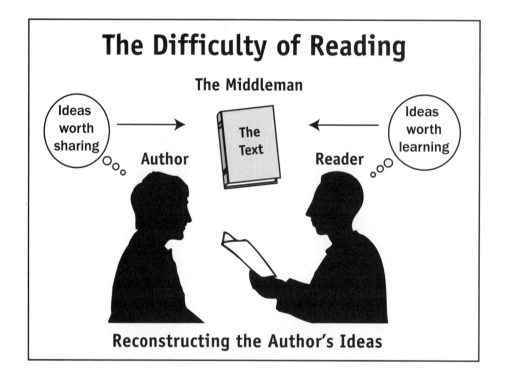

The difficulty for many middle schoolers, as I see it, is that these words, once published and made available to an audience of readers, must stand alone. That is, the reader—a student in our class—has no access to the writer; the writer is not available to the reader to offer clarification, background information, useful asides, or even encouragement. This is very different from a face-to-face dialogue where the spoken words in a conversation are constantly being fine-tuned, elaborated upon, rephrased, and bounced back and forth to increase understanding.

In reading, the words stand alone; they have no backup. Unfortunately—and inevitably—the words can fail to make the thought transfer successful. That is, the author may assume that the reader possesses adequate background knowledge on the topic and therefore skips writing some information—not enough words given. Likewise, the author may select certain words to describe the topic but fail to realize that some readers do not know the meaning of those words—using the wrong words. Plus, the author may use too many words that wear down the reader, or decide not to provide enough supporting graphics, or allow the publisher to chose the wrong font and text size . . . lots of potential interference in the reader-writer communication circle.

But let's not just blame the writer for reading difficulties. The reader, too, can be responsible for miscommunication: A student can read too quickly and miss important cues from the author; read too slowly causing concentration to drift off; allow a tapping pencil from across a classroom to become a distraction; reject the author's communication simply because a teacher assigned it; and many other reader problems that we've seen year in and year out. The reader-writer communication circle gets broken all too frequently.

With all these potential glitches in the writer-to-reader exchange, it's a wonder that comprehension *ever* occurs. At the same time, it's no wonder that many students have turned off to reading. After enough failures at understanding authors' communicated ideas, many readers decide that reading is not their thing, and when the teacher assigns reading in class or for homework, well, thanks, but no thanks. Just as they can with writing, students can grow evasive, resistant, or numb to reading. Or, if they are skilled readers or writers, they may grow lethargic to repeated assignments that do not challenge them.

Let's surprise them. Let's jolt our students awake by providing them with a real reason for writing: to communicate their opinions about a novel, a textbook chapter, a short story, a poem, an article, a Web site, or any reading material back to the author. Reading then serves as a catalyst for the writing. Writing serves as the motivator for reading. The author gives you something to consider, and you write back to the author with something to consider. Just as sixth grader Carissa did. She was inspired to correspond with an author because she had never done so before and she had something important to say. She became aware of the *relationship* between the assigned reading and the author who wrote it for her. She was respected by her teacher when he asked her, and her classmates, to give that author her truthful feedback. Her reading comprehension was strengthened; her writing empowered.

This book is about just that. Linking reading and writing—and the desire to do both—through "talking back" to authors. When we bring the readers directly into the exchange, the communication circle will be unbroken.

With this process, we build the reading-writing connection because this type of feedback-writing requires careful reading; students cannot respond to an author if they fail to understand the author's communicated ideas. Instilling the desire to read carefully in order to respond honestly and accurately makes all the difference. I am in favor of developing good thinking habits in students—critical thinking, analysis, inquiry—to nurture a disciplined mind.

Ideas That Parented This Book

The following is a set of research-based theories that influenced my writing of this book. I share them with you now, so you will understand where I am coming from.

1. **Reading is a transaction.** The notion that the meaning of printed words does not solely reside in those words, but also resides in the mind of the person reading those words, seems obvious to us. But let's give credit to the transactional theory of reading first advocated by Louise Rosenblatt. Her theory gave birth to the *reader response* theory of reading: Each reader has a unique and personal *constructed* response to words on a page. Rosenblatt describes her theory:

   > The special meaning, and more particularly, the submerged associations that these words and images have for the individual reader will largely determine what the work communicates to him. The reader brings to the work personality traits, memories of past events, present needs and preoccupations, a particular mood of the moment, and a particular physical condition. These and many other elements in a never-to-be-duplicated combination determine his response to the peculiar contribution of the text (1938).

   The title of my book draws from this important notion.

2. **The reading transaction is difficult.** As adult, veteran readers we enjoy reading. In fact, we choose to do it for fun. And while some of our students do too, we surely know that some do not seek out reading because the transaction that takes place from the author's words to the reader's mind is not automatic or easy. Rather, it requires work, including the use of key comprehension strategies applied at key moments. Reading comprehension is the meeting of the minds—author's and reader's—and for some young readers, this meeting is elusive. And no doubt due to past struggles with reading, some have become afraid to try. These resistant readers require our help. They need a bigger incentive to take on a reading assignment. That's what this book is about: providing an incentive to read.

3. **Reading comprehension is a process.** In the 1980s I read the work of Professor P. David Pearson, who, among other researchers, was presenting an intriguing idea: Readers follow a process to construct meaning from text. At the time, I was happily employing a process approach in my writing instruction but had not applied such an approach to reading. Since reading and writing always seemed to me to be flip sides of the same communication coin, Pearson's theory made perfect sense. The process, in its generic form, is: 1. prereading, 2. during reading, 3. postreading. No big aha today, but 20 years ago this was a big step forward for me because now I could teach my students a process: what to do to *get ready* to read for a positive head start in meaning-making, what to do *while reading* to support the building of understanding, and what

to do after reading *to solidify and share* the understanding gained from the reading. It's the "what to do" in the reading process that is deeply embedded in this book.

4. **Writing is, of course, a process.** This idea is now so universal that it seems unnecessary to even state it here. But when I began teaching in the early 1970s, I employed, like my own teachers before me, a strict grammar-based approach to writing instruction. Thanks to people like Donald Murray and Donald Graves and their disciples, I, like many other teachers, came to view transcribing thoughts onto paper as a process. Traditionally, the steps in the writing process have been: 1. prewriting, 2. drafting, 3. revising, 4. publishing. All the assignments presented here follow this writing process.

5. **Instruction must be differentiated.** The students in a seventh-grade class may have lots in common, such as age, neighborhood, interests, and teachers. However, they all do not learn the same way or at the same rate. Teachers have always known this, and we've always done our best to address these important differences among learners. Today it's called differentiation, and there are a lot of new ideas about improving our instruction from people like Carol Ann Tomlinson, Diane Heacox, and Rick Wormeli. I draw from their work throughout the book.

6. **Critical thinking skills must be taught directly.** My primary reason for becoming a teacher 32 years ago was to help kids become better thinkers. To me, the most important thing a teacher can do is to teach students critical-thinking skills that will assist them as learners in school and as continuing learners beyond school. I have found that the best way to do this is through literary criticism whereby students critique an assigned reading. I want them to be able to form opinions about the reading, to support and substantiate those opinions, and then to express their opinions in writing. I call it "talking back" to authors. Think of it as literary criticism with a postage stamp.

How to Use This Book

The six chapters are ordered to move your students forward in their ability to read carefully and write forcefully. Chapter 1 addresses the reading-writing connection in fictional selections. I present three writing formats to get your students initiated into this reader-to-writer approach when reading literature.

Chapter 2 uses the same three writing formats to structure reader response, for reading nonfiction. When teaching content areas, such as science, math, or social studies, you can employ the same approach of student-to-author feedback. Students now react to textbooks, articles, Web sites—all kinds of informational texts.

Chapter 3 answers the question "If I take Larry's advice and assign my students to write back to the author, and I really decide to mail the students' work to that author, how can I ensure that their writing will be of a high enough caliber?" In other words,

"How can I get them to revise, edit, and proofread their work, so they are sending their very best writing?" This chapter addresses the challenge of convincing students that revision is not some punishment but rather an opportunity to re-see, revisit, rework a draft in order to get it closer and closer to its intended meaning. I recommend "three rounds of repair" to pull this off.

In Chapters 4 and 5 we consider the "nuts and bolts" of this student-to-author approach. Chapter 4 addresses how to grade student feedback-writing before sending it to the author. I explain how I assess student work, and I introduce you to my favorite scoring device, the ChecBric. Chapter 5 presents solutions to logistical issues for this reading-response approach. First, I share techniques for locating authors' addresses. This is sometimes more difficult than it should be, and I have learned some quick ways to get either e-mail or postal addresses that allow the students to send their feedback directly to the author instead of the slower, and less reliable, route via the publisher. Next, you will get my advice on how to encourage authors to actually write back to your students so that a dialogue develops (and what to do if the author you assign happens to be deceased).

Chapter 6 is for those of you who need an additional set of student-to-author writing assignments—either because you have advanced learners in your classroom who require you to differentiate your instruction or because you have such success with the writing assignments in Chapters 1 and 2 that your students are ready to move into more-complex formats.

The ideas and strategies in this book invite our students—all of them—to join the Club of Readers & Writers. A little "talk back," if you will, to support the crucial skills of reading and writing.

CHAPTER 1

PEEKING BEHIND THE CURTAIN: THE READER'S RESPONSE TO LITERATURE (FICTION)

You should start writing more stories with good sized reading print, lots of information with comedy and laughter, then some pictures. That would be a lot better. You're one great writer, and one long writer. So make it shorter. More people would like it. Trust me.

—Avante, grade 6

I like to surprise students with writing assignments. More accurately, I *need* to surprise students with new, different, inspiring writing assignments to overcome any past negative attitudes toward writing. As teachers we must create motivating, inviting, enticing, tempting, energizing, stimulating, engaging, alluring, and maybe even "fun" assignments to help students to discover the excitement of writing to communicate a real purpose to a real audience.

What constitutes a real purpose and a real audience for middle-school students? How about writing back to the author of a story, novel, play, or poem that the teacher assigned? This audience and purpose are far different than the usual: writing to and for the teacher. Writing to the author requires students to engage with the creator of the text, to analyze what that writer did or didn't do, to critique the author's work. The goal is to help students get involved and invested in their reading and writing.

When a middle school student is assigned to read fiction, the last thing he or she expects to do is to read the story to determine the choices the author has made. Rather, most students assume that after reading, they will be expected to answer questions about the story, do character analysis, complete story webs and maps, or write a book report. Why do they presume all this? Because we have been making these types of assignments for decades.

While I am not advocating that we reject any of these traditional assignments, because they do, in fact, help students grow as writers, I suggest we surprise students by showing them how to peek behind the literary curtain to see what the author is doing. Let's invite students to become members of the distinguished Club of Readers and Writers, a group of literate people who love books—love reading them, writing them, and discussing them.

Author analysis changes a reader's perception of reading. When the reader thinks of the writing as a series of choices made by the writer, the relationship changes. No longer is the reader a passive recipient of the writer's work, a victim of some school assignment. Now the reader becomes a partner, a player in the reading.

Education and behavior expert Alfie Kohn refers to this venture as taking students "backstage." He writes:

> Enhancing skills and disposition are impressive accomplishments, to be sure, but there's something else to be gained by taking children backstage that frankly interests me even more. The third benefit is rarely discussed, possibly because it's inherently more controversial: teaching by doing can change how children regard the activity in question, the people who engage in the activity, and the very idea of authority. It has, in a word, a powerful debunking function (2004).

This idea of "taking students backstage" and helping them become active, critical readers is woven into the lesson ideas that follow.

We'll explore Kohn's notion of challenging "the very idea of authority" in Chapter 6, Advanced Reader-Response Assignments. To begin, though, let's help students peek behind the curtain. In this chapter, we explore six different writing structures with accompanying teaching strategies that assist our students in accomplishing the transition from bored victim in class to an active reader and writer who has something to say to an important person.

These structures are:
- reader-response postcards
- student-to-author memos
- Dear Author letters
- character-to-author memos
- character-to-character memos
- Dear Character letters

Reader-Response Postcards

The first response format, the postcard, is an easy, basic format to start with. Writing a postcard to an author is not intimidating or overwhelming. Rather, students perceive it as easy and doable.

In reality, it's not as easy as it looks. Though short, it still requires literary analysis, critical thinking, opinion making, supporting evidence, and, of course, very careful reading in the first place. The key here is if students think it's easy, then they will proceed with more confidence and energy.

Julie Warner, a high school teacher from Georgia, assigned her ninth-grade remedial reading class to read and respond to the powerful novel *Holes* by Louis Sachar—a popularly assigned book, for many good reasons. Julie added a twist to the post-reading culminating task. She had students write a postcard to Mr. Sachar to give him feedback on his writing.

One of her students, Josh, wrote:

> Dear Mr. Sachar,
>
> I think *Holes* was a great book. I stayed interested throughout the whole story. I liked the fact that the story had a happy ending, but on the other hand, I didn't really like it when you didn't tell what happened to the other boys at the end.
>
> I have a question for you. What gave you the idea for *Holes*? And when can I expect something new from you?
>
> Sincerely,
>
> Josh

Now that Josh has effectively reduced the barrier between himself and a famous author, we should consider how to build on his success to move him further into this territory—to hone his developing analytical skills. While we want (perhaps expect) eighth or ninth graders to write a more complex critique to an author, we must remember that this is a new undertaking for many of our students. The point right now is not to push reluctant readers into deep analysis, but simply to get them to take an initial stab at talking back. So for now, we will celebrate Josh's successful postcard, his success in "reading like a writer"—for straying into the World of Reader Response. Later, in Chapter 6, we will address the possibilities of increasing our students' critical analytical processing with more-advanced writing structures.

TIPS FOR TEACHING SUCCESSFUL RESPONSE POSTCARDS

Here are some pointers to help you teach student-writers to compose a solid basic response to an author:

1. Prompt students to identify positives first.
Ask them to point out
- what they like in the story
- effective literary elements
- helpful characterizations
- descriptive language that allows them to visualize a scene

Ask them also to explain why they like those parts and to offer specific reasons. Have them consider whether the author would like to know that these parts worked for a reader. When they write, they can choose which of their responses will have the biggest impact on the author.

2. Prompt students to identify negatives next.
Ask them to point out
- parts of the story that drag and might even be deleted
- disruptive or annoying literary elements
- character actions that seem unrealistic
- bothersome or confusing language use (specific words or phrases)
- a theme that seems forced or unsupported

3. Teach proper tone of voice.
Have students consider
- how the author might feel receiving a postcard from a reader (Might the author be surprised, pleased, or nervous?)
- their tone when "talking back" (Talking back to authors does not involve rudeness, impoliteness, or inappropriateness. Rather, it requires honesty with politeness and truthfulness with respect, and a commitment to engage in a dialogue, not a diatribe.)
- that they are not writing to a friend (Their tone should be more formal than it is when they write to a friend.)

4. Require students to identify specific examples of likes and dislikes from the story.
Yes, you've already prompted them to do this, but you cannot tell them this enough times. Make sure students can refer to specific examples or places in the text to support their opinions.

Build a set of models for future classes from the postcards students write. Be sure to remove student names and copy a range of examples for contrast.

5. Introduce the assignment with model student postcards.

If this is the first time you're assigning postcards to the author, you may have to compose one (or a few) of your own to serve as examples for your students. (You may also use the student writing in this chapter as models.) Make sure to show a mostly successful postcard rather than a perfect one. Then you can prompt your students to analyze what worked and did not work. Finally, you can say to them, "Can you do better than this one?"

In light of these tips, let's examine another response postcard from a ninth-grade student writer in Julie Warner's class. Felicia wrote:

> Dear Mr. Sachar,
>
> I liked the whole thing except two things. One, when Mr. Sir would pour Stanley's water on the ground. It would have been better if he could have given him lots of water like Mr. Pendarski did. I did not like it when Zig Zag beat up Stan, but I did like when Zero stood up for Stanley. He almost killed Zig Zag . . . .

First, congratulations are in order. This 15-year-old student has pushed her way into the Club of Readers and Writers by addressing a famous author in an honest, truthful communiqué.

Now, let's assess her work based on the tips offered above.

1. She begins with a compliment, a positive comment to the author.

2. She identifies two features that are negatives for her—two decisions the author made that did not work for her as a reader.

3. Her tone of voice is sincere, honest, and polite.

4. She provides specific examples of the negatives (the spilled water and the beating) but gives only a general positive statement: She tells him "I liked the whole thing." (This is an area to build on.)

Once our students have peeked behind the curtain and entered the author's sanctuary, they are in forever. And a good postcard may even elicit a response. Sachar wrote a general letter back to Felicia, Josh, and their classmates, giving them a taste of what it's like to engage in a meaningful written conversation about good literature. This process has prepared them to take another step forward and deepen their responses.

STRATEGIES FOR CULTIVATING STRONG READER RESPONSE

Before we move on to a new response format, let's consider some basic strategies—ways to accelerate students' growth in responding thoughtfully to literature.

✳ **Begin talk-back assignments with short readings.** It is far easier to identify what you like or don't like in a short story or a poem than in a novel or a play. Start simple. If you're looking for short, short stories and poems students will enjoy, some of my favorites are listed at the end of this chapter.

✳ **Tap students' oral language strengths during prewriting activities.** Have students talk about their reactions to the reading. Arrange them in pairs, trios, or groups of four, or gather the whole class for a discussion. (As always, provide clear behavior guidelines and review discussion procedures before you begin. For example, model for them how to briefly summarize a prior speaker's point, how to handle disagreements politely, and how to avoid redundant comments by finding something new to add.)

✳ **Teach students to use reading-response tools.** Use sticky-notes (page 21), two-column response sheets (with columns labeled "quotes from the story" and "my response to the quotes"), or any other note-taking device to support student comprehension during reading.

✳ **Review how to support an opinion.** State your own opinion about something in the reading. Say it to the class without providing any backup support. Ask your students whether they think your opinion will help the author. Prompt them to help you support your opinion by referring to something specific in the story. The key word here is evidence.

✳ **Explain the difference between a basic and an elaborate response.** Tell them that as writers, they have choices to make. They can write a brief, basic, and general response to an author, or they can write a more elaborate, detailed, and specific response. Show them a sample of each or, if none are available, compose one of each on the overhead to model the difference. Emphasize that authors appreciate receiving the latter because it shows genuine interest and respect from the reader.

These strategies help students write effective basic critiques. They also lay the groundwork for more in-depth analysis. You may only want to try the postcard format once or twice and move on to a new response format as soon as students learn to recognize their likes and dislikes in a piece of writing, prioritize their ideas, and write to a new audience, the author, observing a respectful tone. The student-to-author memo is a good next step for students who are new to critical reading and writing.

Using Sticky-Notes to Support Reading Comprehension

A key reading skill is the ability to self-monitor comprehension. Strong readers are able to recognize when they are and are not understanding the author. Weaker readers may have difficulty gauging their understanding and therefore miss important parts of a text without realizing it. And because successful reading comprehension is the obvious prerequisite to successful student-to-author writing, you may need to provide some students with additional support. I recommend sticky-notes.

Most middle-school students enjoy using sticky-notes—they are a novel, colorful, and non-threatening writing material that appeals to visual and tactile learners. They also help kids track their thinking as they read.

When you teach students to use sticky-notes during reading, encourage them to talk back to the author every once in a while (depending on the length of the passage and their reading skills this might mean every few paragraphs or every few pages). As they read, have them jot down a quick response on a sticky-note and post it at the appropriate spot in the passage for reference. Simple questions can help prompt a response.

Some types of responses you might model for students include the following:

REACTIONS
Prompt: What are you thinking about as you read? Did something the author wrote surprise you?

PREDICTIONS
Prompt: What do you think the author might do next in the story? What might the author have this character do next?

QUESTIONS
Prompt: What parts of the story do you find confusing or unclear? What do you want to know more about?

why would he say he was good at racquetball, if he's not he's only going to embarass himself?

A student uses a question response to ask about a character's reaction in one of Gary Soto's short stories, "The Challenge."

UNKNOWN WORDS
Prompt: Do you need to understand this word the author has chosen? If so, what could this word mean? Did the author help out with any content clues? If not, can you do a word-parts analysis to figure it out?

SUMMARY STATEMENTS
Prompt: What important things has the author included so far in the story?

You may want to practice with the class, reading a short story together and stopping at different points to let students try each kind of response at least once. After the reading, let volunteers share their notes or have students share with partners.

Student-to-Author Memos

The most compelling thing about teaching response work with memos is that students have never written one. When informed by their teacher, "After you read this story, please write a feedback memo to the author," students are surprised. Now, most kids may have heard the word *memo*, and some might even know that *memo* is short for *memorandum*, and a few actually might have seen one, but I will bet you that not one of your students has ever *written* a memo. I have asked thousands of teachers in workshops over the years, "Who here has ever assigned memo writing to students?" Typically just one or two teachers among a group of 70 to 80 have. So, it's clear that this assignment is a new one, and this is good news.

We can take advantage of the novelty of this writing structure: Memos get our students' attention. They replicate real-life communication among adults in the workplace, they offer a shorthand structure that students find "cool" (To:, From:, Date:, and RE:), and most importantly, they afford more room to write than a postcard, which encourages a more elaborate response.

Here is a first-draft memo from a sixth grader in Christine Gonzalez's class at East Montana Middle School in El Paso, Texas, to the writer Leon LeWine (my pen name) about the short story "Sidd's Excellent Adventure."

> To: Leon LeWine
> From: Liliana
> Date: Tuesday, November 2, 2004
> Cc: No
> Re: Sidd's Excellent Adventure
>
> I liked how you explained how the cat felt when it was time to go to the vet. I also liked how they felt their emotions. I have four questions: How did you think of a story so nice? Do you have any cats or any other pets? If you do, do you take them to the vet? Do they like the vet? I think that if you want to make your story more interesting you should put a couple of drawings of how the cat would run away or where he would hide, because you could show how it is reacting. Don't forget to color the pictures so they could look nice.

Three components of Liliana's memo impress me:

1. She mentions the specific parts of the story she liked and compliments the author on the way he conveyed emotions.

iliana's advice about adding "a couple of drawings" to my work not only encouraged me to seek out an artist for my story but also has served as a reminder that when I teach reading response, students benefit from visual support while they read. I discovered an excellent during-reading strategy to support visualizing in Eliza Sher's literature class at Sheldon High School in Eugene, Oregon (I also found an artist—student Kelli Sawyer—for my story). Eliza has her students take "SnapShots," or quick sketches, of what they are picturing in their mind's eye as they read. Like sticky-note response posting, SnapShots is a tracking device that supports comprehension and recall. (See page 24 for a lesson on SnapShots.)

2. She asks the author about his motivation and revisits parts of the story that triggered curiosity and questions.

3. She suggests an improvement.

To scaffold her students' writing, Christine provided them with a memo template with a fill-in format. If you're working with reluctant readers and writers, it makes good teaching sense to distribute the memo template early in the assignment, even before students begin to read the assigned fiction. That way, students can use the template as a note-taking tool, to record ideas *while they read*.

TIPS FOR TEACHING SUCCESSFUL STUDENT-TO-AUTHOR MEMOS

Let's add Christine's memo-template idea and Eliza's SnapShot strategy to our Teaching Tips list from the postcard activity.

1. **Prompt students to identify positives first:**
   Ask them to point out what they liked.

2. **Prompt students to identify negatives next:**
   Ask them to point out what they didn't like.

3. **Require them to identify specific examples of likes and dislikes from the story.**

4. **Teach proper tone of voice:**
   Remind them that when they talk back considerately, the author is most likely to listen and respond.

5. **Reinforce comprehension by encouraging students to use during-reading strategies, such as marking ideas in their reading with sticky-notes (page 21), making SnapShot drawings while they read (pages 24–25), and letting students use a memo template to take notes for their response (pages 27–28).**

Using SnapShots to Support Reading Comprehension

A key reading skill is the ability to visualize. Strong readers are able to transpose an author's words into mental images. Weaker readers may have difficulty doing this. And because successful reading comprehension is the obvious prerequisite to successful student-to-author memo writing, you may need to provide some students with additional support. SnapShots is one reliable tool.

> Looking for additional visualization strategies? Check out Jeff Wilhelm's *Reading Is Seeing* (Scholastic, 2004).

For each student, you'll need a copy of a short story, four to six sticky-notes (3 by 3 inches), and a simple booklet to serve as a photo album (several sheets of construction paper folded in half and stapled along the fold). Give students the following introduction:

As you read this story, try to imagine in your mind's eye what is happening. Periodically, I'll ask you to pause in your reading to "take a picture" of what you are seeing in your mind as you read. (You have special SnapShot "film," which I'll give you shortly.) The pictures you take will be quick snapshots, not elaborate works of art. Stick figures are fine. Not every word or sentence in the story deserves a SnapShot. It will be up to you to decide on which scenes are important enough to warrant you drawing one. The number may be three, four, five, or six, or even more—you will decide as you read.

At the end of the period, I will give you a SnapShots photo album. You'll mount your snapshots on the pages and write a descriptive caption beneath each photo.

Then follow these steps:

1. Provide students with a copy of the story and their SnapShot film (the sticky-notes). Optional Alternative: Instead of providing sticky-notes, assign students to draw SnapShots directly onto the photo album. This is the cheaper but also less engaging way to go, as students enjoy drawing on the sticky-note "film" and arranging the SnapShots in the album after they're done.

2. Have students begin to read. Set a timer for 4 minutes to remind yourself to periodically prompt students to pause and draw. Tell them: *Sorry to interrupt your reading, but if you haven't taken a SnapShot lately, now is a good time to do so. You must decide which scene that you've read is important enough in the story to deserve a SnapShot. Snap it quickly—a fast sketch, not a masterpiece.* Let students continue reading and SnapShotting.

3. Have students share their photo albums in pairs, trios, or groups of four so that they have a chance to compare the parts of the story that captured their interest and discover how they may have pictured the story differently or similarly to a classmate. When drawings are very different, encourage students to go back to the story to find the parts that describe the

Using SnapShots to Support Reading Comprehension

SnapShot image. Have them consider whether the discrepancy was caused by an unclear message from the author or by their own reading.

4. Collect and score the SnapShot photo albums. (See assessment ideas on pages 40–42.)

5. You may also want to post the albums on a bulletin board for whole-class sharing.

This is seventh grader Amber's SnapShot of an imagined meeting between two characters from two different short stories, both written by Gary Soto. While reading "The Challenge," in Tom Cantwell's Language Arts class, Amber was reminded of a similar scene in "Seventh Grade," which she read months ago in the class. As she reads, she realizes that in both stories a girl is pursued by a boy, but due to both boys' ineptitude at wooing, both girls are confused by their approaches. Teresa (the character in "Seventh Grade") comments to Estela (the character in "The Challenge") about a scene she liked, but Estela admits she doesn't understand why the boy José no longer speaks to her. Teresa, as an outsider to the story, explains her theory, and Estela thanks her for the clarification. This visualized scene reveals that the student is able to make a connection between two different literary works, which of course is more important than drawing ability.

This SnapShot was taken a number of years ago by Kelli Sawyer, a professional illustrator who was in high school at the time. Kelli Sawyer visualized the narrator of my story "Sidd's Excellent Adventure" as a middle-school-age boy, even though I had not specified the narrator's age or gender. In fact, I intentionally have left this character ambiguous in order to cause readers to make inferences and help readers to take an active role in creating meaning in their own minds as they read. Kelli picked up on certain behaviors as well as language and vocabulary to help her visualize the character.

SnapShot activity description adapted from *Paving the Way in Reading and Writing: Strategies and Activities to Support Struggling Students in Grades 6–12* by Larry Lewin (Jossey-Bass, 2003).

How to Structure a Memo: The Praise-Question-Polish (P-Q-P) Format

Diane Mattison, seventh-grade teacher at Springfield Middle School, Oregon, took my suggestion of assigning student-to-author memos to guide her class. She was impressed with the results and commented, "I chose the memo because it seemed less formidable to students than a letter. I think the goal of being concise and brief in their comments appealed to most kids as well."

Yet some kids wrote an impressive amount. Here is a memo by Alicia from Diane's class:

To: Avi
From: Alicia
Cc: Mrs. Hughes
Date: 11/2/04
Re: The True Confessions of Charlotte Doyle

"Charlotte" was probably the best Newbery Book I've ever read. The diary format made me feel like I was Charlotte. There was so much suspense because of the murders, the trials, and the storm that I couldn't wait to keep reading. The ending was great because Charlotte got to run away and do something she loved. Though I don't usually like "cliffhanger" endings, I didn't mind this one because it was written very well.

Where did you come up with the idea for this story? Were any of the characters based on real people? If so, who, and did you know them? One thing that really interests me is whether or not the Seahawk is real. I'd love to find out because it sounded like an amazing ship. I thought it was mean when the captain put that Charlotte was lost at sea when she was alive. Did that kind of thing ever really happen? The biggest question I have though is, did women ever join crews like Charlotte back then?

There really wasn't anything I disliked about this story. However, one thing did annoy me a little bit. You used the words *commence* and *punctilious* a lot. Actually, I also kind of thought you didn't elaborate on some of the crewmembers' characters. The only other thing was that some of the events, like captain Jaggery dying or Charlotte running way, happened too quickly. Basically, I thought this was a really good book that I would read again. I hope you make some kind of sequel to it.

Not only was Alicia obviously successful here, but so were her ELL peers, whom Diane says, "have a hard time getting into most [reading response] assignments."

Notice that Alicia is following the same format as the sixth graders who wrote me from El Paso: Start with what you liked, move on to questions that caused confusion or stimulated interest, and close with suggestions or recommendations for improvement. This format is the P-Q-P: praise, question, polish. Created by Bill Lyons, a former language arts coordinator from Iowa City and introduced to me by Tom Cantwell, a seventh-grade teacher from Cal Young Middle School, Eugene, Oregon, this structure has proved to be the very best scaffolding I have used to train novice memo writers to organize their critiques for authors.

It offers students a three-paragraph organizational pattern:

Paragraph 1
Praise the author by citing elements, ideas, and aspects of the writing style that you liked. These are the features of the reading that had a positive impact on you as the reader. Complimenting the author requires citing specific examples from the story.

Paragraph 2
Question the author by addressing any confusions that confronted you while reading, any uncertainties, any wonderings about why the author decided to write what he/she wrote. Questions allow you, the reader, to inform the writer about areas that may be causing potential misunderstanding. Of course, citing specific examples from the story is essential.

Paragraph 3
Polish the writing. Offer suggestions to assist the author in improving his or her writing. Here you serve as an editor, providing ideas about how to make the story better for other readers. (This last step bumps up the level of challenge in students' responses because suggesting meaningful revisions requires analysis, evaluation, and synthesis—the highest-order thinking skills on Bloom's Taxonomy.)

SCAFFOLDING STUDENTS' WRITING WITH A MEMO TEMPLATE

Of course, you may be committing "assumicide" if you expect your students to understand and execute a memo-writing assignment with only these instructions: *Write a three-paragraph memo. Your first paragraph will be praises to the author. Your second paragraph will be questions you have for the author. And your third paragraph will offer the author suggestions for improvement.* While these instructions are clear to you, many (perhaps most) students will not get it, and they will end up struggling unnecessarily with this memo assignment. By planning ahead and providing the class with a P-Q-P template, you'll greatly increase students' chances for success.

That's what teachers Theresa Alexander and Susan Aldrich at the Calvary Christian Academy in Philadelphia did for the reluctant readers they work with in their school's resource room. They learned about the P-Q-P memo from me in a course, but they took it a step further by designing a template to assist their students (page 28). You can use this template with your own class or create your own template to meet the needs of your students. You'll find ideas for using the template in the strategies below.

Name _____ Date _____

Memo

To: _____

From: _____

Date: _____

Re: _____

_____

_____

_____

_____

_____

_____

_____

_____

_____

_____

_____

Reminders for Memo:		
P stands for **PRAISE.** Write what you like about the selection (for example: the pictures, wide spaces, clear directions, easy-to-read words). **Sentence Starters** I like . . . It was really neat that . . . That was cool when . . . I agree with . . . I was surprised when . . .	**Q** stands for **QUESTION.** Write any questions you have about the selection (for example: how the author came up with the idea, why the author chose to write a part of the story a certain way, or whether there is a sequel to the story). **Sentence Starters** I was confused with . . . I didn't understand . . . What did you mean when . . . How did you come up with . . .	**P** stands for **POLISH.** Write any suggestions you'd like to make to the author (for example: how to make it more interesting, colorful, or exciting). **Sentence Starters** I would have ended it like . . . I would change . . . I wish that . . . I'm beginning to wonder if . . . I couldn't believe that . . .

E-Memos: Another Easy Format

Ever notice when you compose a new e-mail, it begins with the same format?

From: Christy.G___@___.com

To: larry@larrylewin.com

Date: 10 Dec 2004 14:17:30 -0700

Subject: Your story

Look familiar? It is the memo format, right? Only instead of RE:, the e-mail program uses "Subject." So I've renamed it the *e-memo* for talk-back assignments.

Fifth-grade teacher Craig Smith of New Hope Middle School in Pennsylvania had students compose e-memos to Russell Freedman, author of *Children of the Wild West.*

Send	Save as a Draft	Spell Check	Cancel

<u>To:</u>	Russell Freedman

<u>Cc:</u>	Mr. Smith

<u>Subject:</u>	American Indians

March 18, 2004

Dear Russell Freedman,

I enjoyed reading your book *Children of the Wild West.* I thought it was great how you really had a strong background of how to describe something. Like how you had a picture to show what you were talking about and so you could visualize what the scene looked like. I also thought it was good that you had captions under the pictures so you could tell exactly what you were looking at. I had one question, where did you get all of those great pictures?? By the way, they are all really cool pictures!! I had one suggestion, while I was reading the section on Native Americans I came across a few words that I couldn't pronounce or I didn't know what they meant. Maybe you could try and reword or tell what some of the bigger words mean. Anyway I really enjoyed reading your book and I thought the pictures were great. I really learned a lot about the Native Americans!!

Sincerely,

Marisa

The advantages of e-mail are obvious: rapid delivery, no postage costs, incorporation of computer skills, kid enthusiasm, and increased chances of a reply from the author. Of course, this option requires the author's e-mail address. Where would a student find it? I will offer some suggestions about contacting authors in Chapter 5.

STRATEGIES FOR CULTIVATING STRONG READER RESPONSE

Here are some surefire ways to teach students to use the memo format successfully:

✳ **Link reading and writing with sticky-notes.** To support active student reading, distribute sticky-notes in three different colors. Assign one color for jotting down quick praises while reading, a different color for generating questions, and a third color for polishing suggestions. Not only do color-coded sticky-notes support reading, they provide a bridge to writing by serving as notes for each paragraph in the P-Q-P memo.

✳ **If students need extra support when you introduce memo writing, offer them the reproducible template on page 28.** When you feel confident that students understand the format, remove the scaffolding and let them write their memos on lined paper or the computer.

✳ **Recognize that the space limitations of the template may not accommodate the more elaborate responses you are teaching students to write.** In this case, use the template during the prewriting stage, as a note-taking tool, and later have students write a more expanded rough draft on a larger template, lined paper, or the computer.

✳ **Model how to write solid Praise, Question, and Polish paragraphs.** Also remember to photocopy sample P-Q-P memos from other classes (with names removed) to show on the overhead or as handouts. Discuss how the writing met the criteria for each part and ask students how they might improve the writing.

✳ **To scaffold the paragraph writing further, provide students with sentence starters.** Here are some more to supplement those on the P-Q-P template:

　a. Praises may begin with *I really liked, I appreciated, You were successful when you, I found it interesting that you, I'd like to thank you for, Congratulations on,* and *I was impressed with.*

　b. Questions may begin with *Why, I was wondering why, Did you realize that you, What was your thinking on,* and *Did you intend to.* They may also include comments that point out areas of confusion or concern, such as *I felt somewhat confused by, Your decision to ____ caused me to feel uncertain about . . .*

　c. Polishing suggestions often begin with *I think you should,* but also with *I recommend that you, Would you consider, It occurred to me that maybe you, May I suggest that, I think it might be better if,* and *Perhaps if you . . .*

✴ **Design a customized P-Q-P template to help students meet a particular standard or objective.** For example, as part of a lesson on the use of foreshadowing in a story, you could easily convert the generic P-Q-P format into a more specific one for this literary device: Praise the author's use of foreshadowing. Question his or her use of foreshadowing. Polish—make suggestions for removing, adding, or changing instances of foreshadowing.

✛✛✛✛✛✛✛✛✛✛✛✛✛✛✛✛✛ **Reality Check** ✛✛✛✛✛✛✛✛✛✛✛✛✛✛✛✛✛✛✛

Even with the P-Q-P template, not all students will write high-quality memos. Obviously, the format is consistent, but the actual observations, opinions, questions, and suggestions will vary from student to student. So, keep in mind two things:

First, some student writers will not be able to use the template to create an in-depth, detailed, insightful, interesting, revealing memo to the author. Rather, you should expect a *range* of student responses, from top-flight, to decent, to sadly superficial. Just as with any assignment we create, students will approach it with different abilities, interests, and amounts of energy. Look to the strategies in this chapter for ways to scaffold the assignments and support your most reluctant readers and writers—you may simply need to move on and try another approach to elicit a higher-quality response.

Another point about P-Q-P memos is that, while I love this structure, and many teachers immediately take an interest in using it, not every student will. I have had the disappointing experience of assigning one last P-Q-P memo from the students *to me* evaluating a reading class during the final week only to hear a chorus of groans. Maybe this was due to the late timing of the assignment, maybe it was caused by my overuse of this structure during the course, or maybe some kids just felt they didn't need it anymore. So, we need to be careful with this (or any) writing assignment and use it wisely to gently, but steadily, bump up student critical reading and writing.

DIFFERENTIATING THE MEMO ASSIGNMENT

Let's flashback to the first sample you read, Carissa's memo to me regarding my short story (page 7). Upon rereading it, you will discover that it is a P-Q memo. She praises me for what she likes, and she questions me about some decisions I made. For sixth graders just entering the Club of Readers and Writers, this may be plenty to expect.

Here is one more memo from Mark McKelvey's sixth-grade class:

To: Leon LeWine
From: Michael
Re: Sidd's Excellent Adventure
Date: April 3, 2003

Your story is, to put it simply, fair. There are times of sheer greatness and parts that are difficult to get through without letting your mind wander.

It starts well. It caught my attention as well as my eyes, as I read through the thick punctuation separating the small fragments that made it seem more like an outline than a story. Your beginning, good not great.

Moving toward the middle you begin to fall off-line with a combination of poor word choice and organization. In paragraph three you have a variety of organizational mishaps. In paragraph two you make a poor decision using two consecutive etc. marks. Instead you could have created a wonderful transition from beginning to middle by telling a brief "mini" adventure about catching your cat. Your middle, poor.

As we hit the climax and slow decline toward the peaceful ending, we see great creativity but unconventional, "no" dialog as I would put it, with repeated use of no somethings in place of speech. A flawed climax makes your ending seem hopeless, but you are quickly snatched out by your ultra-neat conclusion. So in that category you get a great. Meaning, good, poor, and great. Leveling out at fair.

Notice the variation in the quality of response. Clearly, not all sixth graders are at the same ability level even though they are all about the same age with the same number of years in school! That's no shock, of course. Every day we teach in classrooms that have a wide range of student abilities, energy levels, and interests. So, let's *plan* on these differences and design our instruction to increase the chances of success for every student. This is differentiating our instruction.

One principle of differentiated instruction (DI) is offering tiered assignments for a class. Carol Ann Tomlinson, the leading U.S. researcher on DI, explains that "tiering is a process of adjusting the degree of difficulty of a question, task, or product to match a student's current readiness level" (2003).

To accomplish this goal and avoid giving all students the same version of the memo assignment, let's review the student-to-author feedback assignments to determine a hierarchy of difficulty. Clearly a P-Q (praise/question) memo is easier for a student to write than a P-Q-P (praise/question/polish), which demands creative thinking. This option creates a two-tiered assignment. You may want to identify which students in a class will be sufficiently challenged by the P-Q memo and assign it to that group. Other students will be better served by the more-sophisticated P-Q-P memo; challenge them with this one. The purpose is to try our best to make every student successful.

Of course, it would be useful to have a third tier ready for those students who can handle a more challenging task such as writing a PreQuel-SeQuel (PQ-SQ) memo (this is essentially an all-Polishing memo). Have students outline suggestions for a prequel and sequel scene for the author to consider adding to his or her work. The memo must include ideas for what happens before the story begins and what happens after the story ends.

Another level-three assignment I have observed in a ninth-grade English class is the Screenplay Adaptation Memo (SAM). In this assignment, students outline their idea for adapting a short story to a screenplay for a possible movie. They write their proposal in a memo to the author with a request to split the royalties should someone in Hollywood like it.

Dear Author Letters

Memos and postcards are great writing formats, but both are relatively short. We can now add the friendly letter to our menu of the student-to-author communiqués. I see author letters as the next level of difficulty following postcards and memos because by providing the most space, letters require more in-depth analysis.

S. E. Hinton, author of the classic novel *The Outsiders*, received book review letters from students in Julie Warner's class. The students had moved on from one-paragraph responses in their postcards to longer, more detailed responses. In this response, Josh needed more room than a postcard or memo would provide to more fully review the novel.

Dear S.E. Hinton

I really liked your novel "The Outsiders." I liked all the characters in the story. They didn't try to impress anyone and didn't care what people think of them. I also like the bad-boy attitude they possessed. Another think I like is that the whole story wasn't violent and you put positive things into the story.

The only thing I can think of that I did not like was the ending. The way Dallas died so soon after Johnny. There wasn't too much that I didn't like. My opinion, you did a good job of writing an interesting book that people want to read.

"The Outsiders" was an interesting book. I stayed into the book the whole time. It really captured my attention. I think my classmates enjoyed the story as well. Everyone liked it.

One of the many things I like about the book was the theme. I really took it to heart and understood it. I also liked the personalities of the characters. Each of them had their own roll in the story.

This was a great book. I enjoyed reading it. You did a real good job on producing a book that will catch the attention of readers. I hope you write again soon.

Sincerely,

Josh

Compare his response to the earlier postcard response to Louis Sachar (page 17). Josh has built writing stamina (he's written five paragraphs to his earlier two) and includes more specific details about what he likes and dislikes (the "bad-boy attitude" of the characters, the timing of Dallas's death, the unique role of each character in the story). His ability and willingness to talk back is developing.

Aside from encouraging length and depth, a friendly letter invites a very personal voice from the writer. A classmate of Josh's wrote a short but insightful letter. It begins with "I know you receive a lot of fan mail, and I know that causes a lot of reading, so I'll try to make this one as short as possible." I like the realization this student has about the author on the other end—a real person with real-life time limitations. A very courteous awareness. I also like how the student does not merely write fan mail—the typical "how I loved the book, you are great, and so on" but rather he/she provides more substance by identifying for the author a specific element of success, her characterization skills. The next line, "But you hear that a lot, don't you?" again impresses me for its friendly intimacy and audience awareness. The ending apology for any disturbance this letter may have caused is a sweet and considerate statement from a student-reader who has entered the author's world through the letter, but who respects a boundary.

That eighth or ninth graders are able to write Dear Author letters does not surprise me. In fact, elementary school students who learn to write well through rich, enjoyable reading and writing experiences can write Dear Author letters that are longer, have better structure, and more depth than this example—I have worked with such students. However, many of our middle schoolers are coming to us with limited and even negative reading and writing experiences and we, like Julie Warner, need to coach them from their comfort zone to new levels that approach grade-level expectations. Below, you'll find strategies for helping students rise to new ability levels in giving critical feedback with letter writing.

STRATEGIES FOR CULTIVATING STRONG READER RESPONSE

What can you teach students about composing a letter that really speaks to the author?

I suggest the following:

✳ **Teach or review the standard friendly-letter format.** While the structure of a letter may be a review for many students, it may in fact be new information to other students. Creating a friendly-letter template (date, salutation, body, closing, and signature) will help communicate your format expectations to the class.

✳ **Review paragraph development.** Because letters are longer, the development of the content must be addressed even more than with postcards and memos. Tell students that each main point they are making deserves its own paragraph. For example, if they are using the P-Q-P format, then they'll write three paragraphs. Explain that each paragraph needs a topic sentence, and each needs several supporting details—evidence from the story that supports your main point. Make sure to model on the board or chart paper how to structure a paragraph.

✳ **Show students how their tone of voice is linked to their audience and purpose.** Remind students that their audience is the actual human being who wrote the story they read. Tell them that this person has no idea how well their reading went. Their purpose is to remove the mystery for the author by explaining their reading experience. This requires a proper tone of voice: friendly yet formal, respectful yet honest, helpful, not punitive. And emphasize for students that it's likely that the author has *never ever* received this type of critical letter from a student. This may be new territory for the author, so they should be aware, sympathetic, and considerate.

> Students will take varying amounts of time to finish writing their letters. If you are using class time to have them compose the letters, invite students who finish before their classmates to make an illustration of a favorite scene in the story to accompany their letter. Or perhaps a student might prefer to draw a new scene or a revised scene to present to the author. In either case, drawing serves to support reading comprehension.

✳ **Provide models of student-written letters.** Just as with postcards and memos, a few examples will greatly support your students in accomplishing this demanding reading-writing task.

More Talking Back: Other Formats for Response to Fiction

Should students always write back to the author or only write to authors? Certainly not. Because, as new, different, and engaging as this assignment is, it eventually can become the same ol', same ol', and a turnoff through overuse.

Let's keep one step ahead of our students and plan on a variation that will build on response skills students have developed with postcard, memos, and letters to authors, but will be different enough to add energy and interest.

CHARACTER-TO-AUTHOR MEMOS

This reading-writing assignment is an obvious cousin to the student-author memos. The difference is that the student plays the role of a character in the assigned fictional reading rather than write from a student-reader stance. This invites students to explore character development and motivation and author intention.

Students "get into character" and write to their author to do the following:
- compliment her or his portrayal of "me, the character"
- complain about decisions the author made in writing that reflect badly on the character
- challenge or question the author (e.g., "Why are you saying this about me?")
- suggest changes in the plot to better present the character or make the character's life easier, more interesting, challenging, and so on

CHARACTER-TO-CHARACTER MEMOS

You might modify the above assignment by switching the audience from the author to another character. Now the student takes on the persona of a character in the assigned fictional reading and communicates with another character in the form of a memo— an insider-to-insider communiqué that is another entry point for students to explore character development.

Here are some ways to focus a character-to-character memo assignment. Have students write as one character addressing another character in one of these:
- an upfront appraisal of the other character's actions, attitudes, or plans
- a complimentary note expressing praise for what the character has done
- a rebuke for an error in judgment
- an apology for a misunderstanding
- an offer of a truce over a disagreement
- a suggested plan to accomplish a mutual goal
- an FYI revealing information as yet unknown by the other character
- a prediction about what might happen to them later in the story and what to do about it

You may find many other angles on your own and by asking students what they think any two characters in a story might want to discuss.

"DEAR CHARACTER" LETTERS

If you are seeking a format for a deeper, more extensive character analysis, try this adaptation, created by Heather Scheiber of Wantagh High School in New York. Heather decided to have her ninth graders write a reader-to-character letter to help them read more deeply into Sophocles's *Antigone*. Her assignment is for her students to write to Antigone to offer helpful advice. This assignment pushes her students very deeply into the literature, way beyond a more traditional character-analysis piece.

Here are the directions Heather gave her students:

You've just finished reading the first scene of Antigone. *Now you understand her dilemma: Should she bury her brother or not?*

Write a note to slip under Antigone's door tonight before she runs out the door with a shovel! Keep it short and sweet. Ask yourself:
- *What advice do you want to give her?*
- *Can you persuade her to follow your advice?*

Her student Kristina wrote this short letter in response:

Dear Antigone,

I'm sorry to hear about your brothers. I know it's tough to deal with, but I feel that you are a very strong person and both you and your sister can get through it together. I agree with you, I would definitely want to give ANYBODY I love a proper burial. Especially my brother. I think that if you do plan to bury your brother, try to do it at night, that way there is a slight chance that you wouldn't get caught. I think you are very brave to go against your uncle. I also think that you shouldn't hate your sister just because she's not on your side. She's only watching out for you, be thankful that she doesn't tell anybody about you burying your brother. But I know that if I was in your situation I would have done the same. But Antigone, you must also think of the consequences. If you do get caught you will die. But I'd rather die trying than not doing anything at all. Follow your heart.

My deepest sympathies,

Kristina

Not only does Kristina follow the assignment instructions, keeping her letter short and offering the character sound advice in the face of danger, she writes with a distinct voice. We can appreciate the degree of connection Kristina feels—we hear the empathy that drives her analysis. My guess is that this work of literature will live on for her far longer than it would have had she answered an essay question.

TIPS FOR THE "DEAR CHARACTER" ASSIGNMENT

To replicate this assignment, let's consider a few points that can make or break our students' success. We can do the following:

✳ **Establish a purpose for reading.** Before they write to a character, tell the class right up front why they are reading the assignment: to analyze a character, to get into that character's life, and to make helpful suggestions, recommendations, and insights into the character. This paves the way for the writing assignment.

✳ **Provide students with a clear focus for their writing.** In Heather's "Dear Antigone" letters (above), her students were directed to give the character advice on deciding on the next action. Very clear.

✳ **Help students decide on an appropriate writing style and tone.** Ask students how formal the style should be. Will they approach this writing to the character as a friend-to-friend letter, or a student-to-adult letter, or a knowing reader–to–clueless character letter? Each is a legitimate approach; kids just need to think about which way to go and why. The language, sentence structure, and tone of voice will all be affected by their decision.

✳ **Remind them that the more information from the reading they incorporate into their character letter, the better.** Tell them that clear references to what happened in the story will anchor their communication to the character and help them keep their focus.

> ### Writing to Dead Authors
>
> Rather than having our students always write to us, it is better to occasionally surprise them with a real audience—even a real dead one. I find that students don't mind at all.
>
> However, deceased authors cause a logistical problem—it is difficult to mail the memos to them! I will address this potential glitch in Chapter 5.

✳ **Set an appropriate goal for the length of the letter.** Most reluctant writers want to know "How long must my character letter be?" Heather instructed her class to keep it "short and sweet." Another answer is "Long enough to meet the assignment's objectives." So, when discussing a writing assignment's length, I like to review the objectives rather than to say, "One to one-and-a-half pages double-spaced." Better yet, design and distribute a checklist or rubric with the assignment's targets, and go over each one with the class. (See my combined ChecBric idea on page 40–42.)

Connecting the Reader-Writer Circle

Think back to the diagram in the Introduction showing the difficulty of reading (page 10). It illustrates how readers must perform the challenging task of re-creating the intended meaning from the writer's words—quite a difficult task because the author is nowhere in sight to better explain, elaborate, or defend the expressed ideas, opinions, or events. Once the writing is published, the writer drops out of the communication loop and leaves the reader alone to figure it out. The reader-writer communication circle gets broken.

I say let's reconnect that circle by inviting the author back into the exchange by mailing the memos, postcards, or letters to that author. By sending student feedback to the author we are mending the severed line between reader and writer.

Of course, this suggestion creates a few logistical problems for us.

1. If our students are really going to send their feedback to published authors, we had better build in some quality editing time so that their writing represents their best effort and ability. The last thing I would want as a teacher is for my students' errors, inaccuracies, or sloppiness to embarrass them in front of an important author. (Actually, I wouldn't want to be embarrassed by my students' carelessness.) But editing, rewriting, and proofreading take time and most students are not particularly excited about this part of the writing process. How do we pull this off?

   To be honest, not every postcard, letter, or memo assignment I collect from students gets mailed off to the author. It all depends on how much time I have and which purpose I am prioritizing. If writing postcards to the author succeeds in motivating students to read, often we just keep them as rough drafts in the classroom. But for the responses that I do send to an author, I employ a three-stage *repair process* (revision) that I explain in Chapter 3.

2. We somehow must locate authors' addresses so that students' responses can actually be sent. Is there a better way than mailing them to the publisher's address and hoping for the best?

   With the advent of the Internet and World Wide Web, I have gotten pretty good at finding both e-mail and postal addresses for authors, so that I can avoid the publisher as the middleman. I will share my Internet tips in Chapter 5.

3. When students have taken the time and expended the effort to write and rewrite a response to an author's work, they typically expect to receive word back from the author addressing their feedback. How do we get busy professional authors to take the time to write back to our students—to complete the circle of communication?

   I have found that it is smart for teachers to provide the author(s) with a heads-up that we have students who have written postcards. If the author knows they are coming, it greatly increases the likelihood of a response. Again, the Web can be very helpful here, and we will check it out in Chapter 5.

   But now, it's time to address the issue of assessing the postcards before the author lays eyes on them. How can we fairly, accurately, and quickly give our students feedback on their "talk backs" to an author? How can they determine areas in need of improvement? With a ChecBric, of course.

Assessment Time

Before mailing the postcards, memos, or letters to the author, we must first assess them. I recommend using a ChecBric to evaluate student writing. This evaluation tool helps you determine how well students are meeting the assignment's objective of responding critically. You can use it to assist them in polishing their writing before mailing it to the author.

What is a ChecBric? It is a hybrid scoring device that combines elements of a checklist and a rubric: *Chec* + *bric*. (An example of a P-Q-P ChecBric appears on page 41.) I prefer ChecBrics to rubrics simply because students find them easier to use. The problem with rubrics, I've found, is that they often overwhelm our students. They are usually too long, they use teacher language, and they are too busy-looking.

Instead, a ChecBric combines the best elements of the rubric:
• a list of the key components (traits) of an assignment
• a scoring point-scale for more objective grading

with the best elements of a checklist:
• bulleted requirements of an assignment spelled out in language students can understand, such as the use of the term *target*, rather than *trait* to name the assignment's objectives
• check boxes for students to mark as they meet the requirements

The checklist is set in the left column and space is provided at the bottom so that students can write a reflection on their work. I give students three suggestions for using the checklist side before, during, and after they write:

1. Look it over *before* beginning to write for a heads-up on the assignment's requirements.

2. Use it to check off the requirements *while* you are writing.

3. Double-check *after* writing to be sure you actually did what was required.

Then I tell them to staple (or paperclip) their ChecBric to their writing, so I can use the rubric side to circle a score they earned for each of the traits.

When you adapt or design your own ChecBrics, remember to use student-friendly language on the student checklist side and keep the targets you assign to a manageable number—three or four is usually enough. Also, provide room for students to reflect on their performance. For example, when you introduce the ChecBric to a class, give students examples and sentence starters such as *what I like about my postcard, what was difficult for me with the postcard,* or *what I might do differently with another postcard*

Name _____ Date _____

Praise-Question-Polish ChecBric

Student Checklist

Target 1: Praise the author.

- ❏ I tell what I like about the writing.
- ❏ I explain why I like it.
- ❏ I give specific details from the reading.

Target 2: Question the author.

- ❏ I ask for more information.
- ❏ I ask for clarification.
- ❏ I ask why the author made certain choices.

Target 3: Make suggestions to the author for polishing.

- ❏ I suggest ways to improve the writing.
- ❏ I explain why my suggestions will make the writing better.

Student reflections on the assignment:

_____

_____

_____

_____

_____

_____

_____

_____

_____

Teacher Rubric

Trait 1: Compliments the Author

4 = Advanced: insightful and compelling positive feedback

3 = Proficient: decent and helpful positive feedback

2 = Basic: overly broad or general positive feedback

1 = Below Basic: unclear or simplistic positive feedback

Trait 2: Seeks Clarifications

4 = Advanced: deep, insightful, or profound questions

3 = Proficient: adequate, interesting, or useful questions

2 = Basic: obvious, generic, or commonplace questions

1 = Below Basic: limited, naive, or irrelevant questions

Trait 3: Makes Recommendations

4 = Advanced: strong and insightful recommendations

3 = Proficient: standard, adequate recommendations

2 = Basic: inadequate, obvious recommendations

1 = Below Basic: limited or trite recommendations

Teacher comments to student:

_____

_____

_____

_____

_____

_____

_____

_____

_____

assignment in the future. This gives you insight about their successes and struggles as well as about what makes them tick—insights you can draw upon to guide instruction. Use the area at bottom right of the ChecBric to write a comment to each student to supplement the circled scores.

ENCOURAGING STUDENTS TO SELF-ASSESS

You may need to modify the ChecBric to better meet the needs of your students and teaching goals. Here's a great way to incorporate self-assessment: Tell students that they are to use the left side, but if they'd like to "peer over the fence" to the teacher's side and circle the score for each trait they predict they've earned, they are welcome to do so. This suggestion, from a teacher who attended my workshop, is excellent because it moves students from being assessed to self-assessment—a goal many teachers have for their students. Of course, many students may optimistically circle higher scores than they will actually earn, so plan on setting aside some time for one-on-one debriefing to explain why they earned what they earned. I often tell students, "It is great that you were shooting for a 4 on this target, but to earn a 4 next time, you will need to. . . ." And I point to the bulleted requirements while explaining the degree of performance.

Of course, you are welcome to modify the ChecBric in any other way to better meet the needs of your students. Feel free to use the reproducible template or design your own.

What to Do When Students "Just Want to Be Left Alone"

While all these response formats, strategies, and tips, plus any others you or your students create, are excellent for motivating critical reading and inspired writing, none is powerful enough to cause all students in every class to become outstanding readers and writers.

Old friend and veteran teaching colleague Roscoe Caron told me a story about his student-teaching days. He was a very energetic student teacher who constantly planned assignments that challenged his students. His cooperating teacher, a woman he greatly respected, supported and mentored him, but finally one day responded to another of his ideas with, "Roscoe, why don't you just leave the kids alone! It's okay to use a worksheet once in a while because they actually like doing routine work!"

Good point. Many students may prefer more mundane school assignments because they know how to do them (or how to go through the motions of doing them).

So, we'd better address this issue: What to do when students "just want to be left alone"?

1. Incorporate traditional assignments into our instruction. There is no need to abandon guided-question worksheets, fill-in-the-blank exercises, book reports, and other literal-level assignments if they assist student learning and provide you with information about their progress. We just want to minimize over-reliance on these assignments to provide critical-reading instruction.

2. Tell them that "talking back to the author" is more difficult than the usual assignments they get, but you will promise to help them succeed. Assure them that you will provide a support structure to help them think through the assignment (you might offer reading support strategies, such as ways to mark texts with sticky-notes and writing scaffolds such as templates), that you'll show them in advance how they will be evaluated (with a ChecBric), and that you'll visit them one-on-one at their desks to check in with their progress. If you can foster a "we're in this together" atmosphere, self-assurance goes up and lack of confidence goes down.

3. Inform them that this assignment is an experiment. If this is your first attempt, tell them that you've never tried this type of reading-writing with any other class, but you have a good feeling about this class's ability, and you think they can pull it off. A little flattery induces self-confidence and energy.

4. Offer them a choice of assignments: Let each student decide what degree of difficulty he or she wants to pursue. Create a menu of writing assignments from recall-and-regurgitate tasks, to more demanding compare-and-contrast work, to a tough analysis and critique. You can encourage students to challenge themselves by offering more points for the more challenging assignments.

Reading fiction is a lovely enterprise. Many of us read novels, short stories, and poetry for the sheer enjoyment of sharing the author's portrayal of the human condition. But if a reader doesn't already know about fiction—what it is, why it's written, that it is enjoyable as well as revealing—then the joy may be missing. If the joy is missing for students in our classrooms, we need to do something, and we need to do it quickly.

Talking back to authors is a means of converting reading-because-I-have-to into reading-because-I-matter. Communicating back to a person who has attempted to communicate with them changes students' attitudes. It puts purpose in the forefront of reading. It is different from the standard postreading activities we have used for decades. While these typical assignments still have value, I have suggested we balance the comfortable and the traditional with the new and experimental.

And because we know better than committing instructional "assumicide," we provide our students with writing structures that assist them in framing their reader responses.

From the short and easy postcard to the cool-looking memo and its adaptations to the more elaborate friendly letter, we can offer guidance as they compose their thoughts.

The same thing can happen when students are assigned nonfiction, informational-text reading. Reading this genre of writing is tough-going for many students. The next chapter addresses how to help them muster the energy and skills to read, comprehend, and respond critically to articles, textbooks, directions, or biographies.

Recommended Short, Short Stories and Poems

Gary Soto, *Local News*. (Harcourt Brace Jovanovich, 1993): 15 fabulous short stories starring middle-school-age protagonists.

Poetry 180, Library of Congress: 180 poems for middle and high school students selected by Billy Collins, a former poet laureate. Available online: http://www.loc.gov/poetry/180

Larry Lewin, assorted short stories. I am nowhere near the league of the above writers, but my stories are short, and they are free at my Web site: http://www.larrylewin.com/books

CHAPTER **2**

QUESTIONING AUTHOR(ITY): THE READER'S RESPONSE TO NONFICTION TEXTS

Even though your article was good, it really didn't

have enough information for our whole class. We

needed to go through a lot of sources to get all

the information we needed. . . . It was REALLY

hard to find the information that you didn't give

us. . . . Your work is almost adequate.

—Adriana, eighth grade

Imagine a student who dislikes reading the math textbook. I know this is a wild fantasy, but just try.

Now imagine the teacher who resents being blamed for the "boring" book, as if he were the author who spent weekends and vacations writing the most torturous text possible. And picture not just one dissatisfied customer but many students in the class complaining.

The teacher, of course, is not the author of the math textbook, and in fact was not even responsible for selecting it. He inherited it when he was hired to teach sixth grade, and he believes it suffices for the most part. But he is aware of the student-textbook disconnection, and it bothers him. Can he do anything to reconnect the student-author circle?

Structured Student Venting: Postcards and Memos Written to Textbook Authors

Dave Smith, a teacher at Briggs Middle School in Springfield, Oregon, decided to let his students vent their dissatisfaction by talking back to the textbook company in a memo. Student-to-author memos, as described in Chapter 1 (pages 22–23), serve as a solid structure for students who are new to critical reading and writing.

Sam, a sixth grader in Dave's math class, was eager for the opportunity.

To: Scott Foresman—Addison Wesley
From: Sam
Re: 6th grade math book

I give this book a 3 out of 10 because to me it lacks everything I would want: algebra with candy, animal cartoons to express certain mathematic terms.

The book needs a new cover—something catchy, not some boring scuba diver & a dolphin. It could use more description on the mathematic terms, but have some fundamental ways to learn math.

—I say it's a Snoozefest (boring)!!

Let's assess Sam's feedback:

1. He rated the text on a 10-point scale.

2. He provided specific areas in need of improvement.

3. He used language well (e.g., ". . . to *express* certain mathematical terms," "a *catchy* cover," "*fundamental* ways" to learn math, and "it's a *Snoozefest.*")

Sam's thinking is revealed in his critique. He went beyond simply rejecting the book with a superficial comment like "this book stinks" or "I hate this dumb book." He thought about his math textbook in an entirely new light. Of course, I would like more information about his opinions of the textbook, as would Dave, his teacher. We'd like to hear from him about the effectiveness of the book's layout and design, the appropriateness and number of the examples offered, the readability and complexity of the writing, and perhaps an admission that at least one aspect of the book worked for him. And once he's had more experience with writing critiques, we can expect him to construct an elaborate, cohesive, analytical critique of a textbook.

WRITING TO AUTHORS OF NONFICTION

Notice that the audience of Sam's memo is the publisher, not the actual authors, which is a reasonable alternative: We can send student reactions right to the top. However, I prefer having students write to the authors directly so that they make a person-to-person rather than a person-to-company exchange.

Writing directly to the author(s) reminds students that books—even those that students may view as boring—are written by people who have something to share with other people. In the example above, a group of college professors with expertise in mathematics want to share their expertise with developing math students. While it's perfectly obvious to us, it usually comes as a total surprise to students to think of their math book (or any textbook) in this way. It changes their perception of it from a sacred, if burdensome, tome created at the beginning of time, hatched in the school's library some stormy night during vacation and finally passed on to them as a form of ritualistic punishment. Instead, students who write to textbook authors come to see their textbook as a series of choices made by human authors, decisions made to best pass on the knowledge of mathematics. That's a big difference.

To initiate this change of heart, I recommend early in the year, or the semester, when you first distribute a textbook, encourage students to get up close and personal with the lead author, so they feel comfortable appraising the writing. Instruct students to open the book to the title page and find the names of the lead author and the university with which he or she is affiliated. They might even examine the author's photograph, if it's included. I continue to break down the barrier between students and the textbook by referring to the author by name as I teach—*What do you think Jeanine was intending to happen when she gave this example on page 127?*

The ultimate goal of increasing students' connection with the author is to improve their content learning. When we establish a connection between the learner and the learned, the novice and the expert, students feel less alienated and victimized as learners. We want to elevate their status in order to inspire them to become more active participants in their learning. And because the textbook is a tool, often the main tool, in their learning, we need to help (and motivate) students to use that tool effectively.

Providing a well-supported critical-analysis writing assignment that puts students in the position of critic is the catalyst—reading, thinking, and learning are the outcomes. And students can use their writing to communicate with and be recognized by published authors—perhaps even get their ideas published. Sam's teacher Dave Smith e-mailed me, "By the way, [my] students are super excited about your request to include their memo responses in your book. Thanks for helping me change lives!"

I provide more ideas on contacting authors and publishers to share students' writing with its intended audience in Chapter 5.

Textbook Feedback Postcards: A Model Lesson

Laura Scruggs, a colleague of Dave Smith's at Briggs Middle School, also wanted her students to cross the divide between student and expert. She chose the postcard format to provide her seventh-grade students with an outlet for their opinions about their social studies text. Introduced in Chapter 1 for responding to literature (pages 17–20), this format also works for responding to informational text.

Laura's own frustration with the textbook's coverage of the Middle Ages prompted her to have students use other sources first and then read and critique the social studies textbook. She comments, "Our textbook has just three pages on the entire European Middle Ages. It includes three paragraphs on the Black Plague and no feudal pyramid"— elements she thinks are critical to students' understanding of the period.

The steps Laura's class took in responding to the textbook include the following:

1. studying the topic from other sources, including the library, Internet, teacher resources, and activities

2. reading the section on the topic in the textbook when their research was almost finished

3. evaluating the coverage provided by the textbook (Laura's students asked, "Where's the rest [of the information]?")

4. using their responses around this question as material for the response postcard

To pull off this assignment with a diverse group of students, Laura used flexible, temporary groups. She split the class into two groups: students who had passed the unit test and students who needed to study for the retest. Before grouping her class, Laura explained the student-to-author feedback assignment and introduced the P-Q-P writing format (pages 26–27). She asked the first group to cluster together, pulling their desks into a circle, and to follow her instructions to write a postcard. This arrangement allowed them to seek help from one another when they had writing questions while Laura worked with the other group.

Laura led the second group through a review of the chapter. Periodically she visited the independent group to check on their postcard progress, answer questions, and urge them onward.

A few days later, after the second group took the chapter retest, they also wrote postcards to the textbook's author. The first group reviewed the postcards they had written earlier and then advanced to another assignment: to examine the sets of social studies textbooks the teachers were considering adopting next year. The book samples happened to be in Laura's classroom, and she had some extra copies of the evaluation form she and her colleagues were using.

After her students had written their postcards, Laura invited them to add an illustration they thought the authors of the textbook should include in their chapter. This also helped students process important ideas in their reading (for other visual techniques to support comprehension, see Chapter 1, pages 24–25).

Here is a fine example of a postcard from the class:

> This is a great example of differentiated instruction method known as a "sidebar" activity: Students who have mastered the concepts and finish early are given a task that is related to the original activity but takes them on a lateral path of learning, rather than moving them forward and separating the class.

November 24, 2004

Dear Dr. Richard G. Boehm,

I really liked the section of "life in the Middle Ages" (pg 311). I think that putting maps and photos are really good for making the text clear. Your system of doing vocabulary is awesome because it's easy to find the definitions. Your writing is very understandable. I like how you had question after the writing.

What made you get the idea to write a social studies book? What made you put it in the order it is in? What made you choose the pictures [you] put in it? How long did it take to get the book done?

I think that you should have used more pictures. If you use more detail and had more information maybe more age groups could read the book. I think you should talk more about the Magna Carta. I would be delighted if you take your time to write me back.

Sincerely,

Tyler

The student-to-author postcard assignment is designed to increase student stamina and capacity for writing, and it worked for Tyler. He also followed the three-paragraph Praise-Question-Polish (P-Q-P) format described in Chapter 1.

1. His introductory paragraph compliments the author on four elements of the text that helped him learn about "Life in the Middle Ages."

2. Tyler's second paragraph asks the author questions that get to the heart of the author's decisions, and he wonders about the author's writing process.

3. The final paragraph provides his suggestions for improvement, including the typical request for more pictures, but also the desire for more information.

Tyler's concluding line "I would be delighted if you take your time to write me back," is a plea for continuing the reader-to-writer exchange. Imagine a sixth grader begging for a dialogue with his textbook's author! How could he ever read a textbook again without thinking about that book's writer and the writing decisions he or she made? Tyler has become a permanent member of the Club of Readers and Writers.

Tyler's classmate Kailey also wrote to Dr. Boehm. Her second paragraph reveals critical reading by pointing out areas of difficulty for the reader/learner:

> Some of your info was very hard to read because of the huge words. The section on disaster and change doesn't give me enough info and the sentences are a little confusing. In that section there isn't a lot of detail . . . your illustration of the "Scale of Effect of the Bubonic Plague in England" is confusing because we have to estimate what it would be.

Tyler and Kailey's ability to make critiques with specific page and title references indicates that they read the chapter on "Life in the Middle Ages" and *read it carefully*. Indeed, students doubly benefit by this assignment: They read to understand and write to deepen their learning.

STRATEGIES FOR CULTIVATING STRONG READER RESPONSE

Let's consider some steps to follow to promote successful student critical feedback to their nonfiction reading assignments.

✳ **Provide structured reading support to aid students' comprehension.** The better students comprehend their assigned reading, the more substantive their feedback to the author will be. Just as with fiction reading, you can employ note-taking and visualization strategies, such as concept drawings, to help students track their understanding while they read nonfiction texts. See also the strategies described in Chapter 1.

✳ **Introduce the audience and purpose of the assigned writing.** Especially if writing in response to nonfiction texts is new to your students, clearly state why you're asking them to write to the author(s). Explain that as students, they are the consumers of the information presented, and they deserve the chance to tell the author(s) their opinions. Show them how feedback includes both positive comments and constructive criticism with specific examples. Teach them about proper tone of voice. (See Chapter 1 for tips on teaching these elements, pages 18–19.)

✳ **Provide a simple organizational structure for students to follow.** Whether you choose to assign a postcard, a memo, or even a longer letter format, offer students a compelling, easy-to-follow structure. I prefer the P-Q-P format, but you may want to work with others. These structuring ideas are organized from least- to most-challenging:

Bullet-Point Format
- Report card (letter grades are given on various categories with explanations)

Two-Paragraph Format
- Liked and Didn't Like (what I liked and what I didn't like about your chapter or article)
- Glows and Grows (positives and areas in need of improvement)
- Keepers and Kick-Outs (what you should keep and what you should delete)
- Inject/Reject (what you should add and what you should delete)

Three- and Four-Paragraph Format
- Three Must-Know Things (three things you need to know about your chapter or article)
- P-Q-P-R (Praise-Question-Polish critique that includes a student-written Rewrite sample that makes an improvement to the original)

Students may also need a template to help them replicate this structure and guide their writing (see the reproducible template on page 28).

Using Concept Drawings to Support Comprehension

Wisely, Laura Scruggs structured her students' reading about the Middle Ages in their social studies textbook with a visual thinking activity. She taught them how to draw a "feudal pyramid" that represents the social order of feudal society, and she assigned her students to create a comic strip version of the chapter. Both of these helped them conceptualize what they read and absorb more information about the Middle Ages. At right is one student's feudal pyramid drawing.

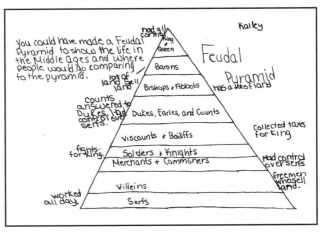

If developing readers in your class lack the ability to visualize ideas and concepts presented in texts, they will need some support in learning how to translate the author's words into mental images. (See also the SnapShot strategy described in Chapter 1 and the professional sources for teaching other visualization strategies listed there.)

✳ **Show, don't just tell, students what you expect from their writing.** Carol Ann Tomlinson, author of many great resources on differentiated instruction, said in a conference on DI, "It is not necessarily obvious to all kids even though we made it perfectly obvious. Make very explicit what you thought, assumed, hoped was very implicit" (2003). For response writing, this involves two techniques.

- First, show students examples of response-writing assignments that are written around their grade level. If you have copies of talk-back assignments from previous classes, use them. If not, write a few yourself. I recommend providing several models that represent a range of quality. Have students critique the weaknesses and defend the strengths of each piece and decide what they would do differently.

- Second, review with students the assessment tools you plan to use. Students need to know in advance what will be required of them, and how they will be assessed. I like using a ChecBric to accomplish both (see Chapter 4).

✳ **Plan time for students to produce several drafts of their writing.** To build writing skills requires multiple trials. If you want students to produce quality written work, they will need enough time to revise. The writing process is time-consuming, as we all know, but it is designed for writers to get closer and closer to what they are thinking—fine-tuning the thought process. Of course, we always must balance the need for revision with the demands of time. We may never be able to pull off enough

+++++++++++++++++++++ **Reality Check** +++++++++++++++++++++

Don't be concerned if you find that students have more polishing suggestions than positive comments for a textbook author. While the Praise-Question-Polish format requires students to begin with something positive in the praise section, some of them—particularly older students—seize the opportunity to unload on a book they don't like in the polish section.

My advice is the following:

1. Let's not allow our feelings to be hurt. We may like the textbook just fine, but we should remember we are not the book. Don't take any criticism of it personally.

2. Teach students that their criticism must be substantiated. If students find fault with a book or an article you assign, that's good. We want our students to develop critical-thinking skills. But to develop these skills, they need to learn how to support their opinions with evidence from the source—another key skill. Alert students that comments like "Your book is boring" or "This article makes no sense" cannot be sent to the author until they go back to the reading assignment to locate examples that support the opinion and then insert them into the critique (see Chapter 3 for more detail on student editing techniques).

revision to produce perfect talk-back writing, and that's okay. You'll find more ways to guide students in the revision process in Chapter 3.

✳ **Mail students' responses to the author.** Once students have revised their work and you are pleased (or at least satisfied) with the results, go ahead and mail them to the author. This shows students that you are serious about talking back. Chapter 5 provides logistical help with contacting authors.

Planning for Degrees of Difficulty in Response Writing

When you plan reading-response assignments, you may want to consider student feedback to authors, publishers, or any other authority, in a taxonomy of response. This framework can help you achieve two goals: to recognize and respect current student ability levels, as well as to eagerly, but gently, push students toward higher developmental levels.

I base my lessons on three levels, in ascending order of difficulty.

THREE LEVELS OF WRITTEN RESPONSE
1. Rating the Author's Work
2. Critiquing the Author's Work
3. Improving the Author's Work

Rating the Author's Work

Rating the author's work is the most basic level of reader response; therefore, it is the easiest and most common response for our students. Rating an author can take various forms, including these:

• general comments such as, "Your story was the best (or worst) I've ever read." Or, "This book is boring" and "I didn't like the ending."

• a basic rating system such as the 10-point or four-star scale or letter grades

Rating an author's work is a useful starting point for coaching students to offer feedback on their reading. Keep in mind that rating will produce a superficial response if the assignment doesn't demand that students provide reasoned support for the comments they give or the scores or grades they assign to the writing.

Critiquing the Author's Work

At the next level of response, students must analyze, evaluate, and appraise what worked and what didn't work in the writing and most importantly, explain why. This assignment requires more information from the student-reader and a more detailed defense of his or her opinion. Critiquing the author elevates students' thinking from "what I like and don't like" to Bloom's evaluation level.

Critiquing can even help students explore a piece of writing at the highest level of analysis: identifying choices the author has made and considering possible reasons for those choices. They may recognize the author's point of view on the topic, contrast elements the author included with those that the reader expected (or found in another resource), and pinpoint examples of bias, misinformation, and error. This type of response resonates with Kohn's expectations that we foster student skepticism of school resources, an idea we'll revisit in Chapter 6.

Improving the Author's Work

At the third level of response (suggestions to improve upon the author's work), students not only analyze and evaluate the author's choices, they also synthesize their learning from the reading. Now they must make specific recommendations for improving the quality of the writing for other readers: Students are *reframing* the author's original work. Now the student-reader serves as an editor or even a coauthor, taking what the author wrote and determining what should stay as is, what should be expanded or contracted, what should be relocated, and what should be deleted. All suggested changes must be accompanied by a clear explanation, a rationalization on why this would be preferable to the original. I suggest supporting students who are ready to respond at this level with the P-Q-P-R (Praise-Question-Polish-Rewrite) format (see pages 26–27).

THE MATH TEXTBOOK POSTCARD IN THREE LEVELS

I often use the three levels of written response to create a differentiated assignment that matches up with the variety of learners I have in a class. Recently, I designed three tiers of reader-response postcards to a math textbook and typed them onto "task cards" for students. Here are the three tiers:

Task Postcard # 22T

RATE THE CHAPTER

Write a postcard to Professor Ron L., head author of your math textbook *Middle School Math, Course 3*, telling him **the grade/score he earned** for writing Chapter 2, Integer Operations.

Rate the chapter to show how well it has helped you learn about adding, subtracting, multiplying, and dividing integers.

To rate the chapter, you will need to design a rating system. For example, you may use

- the A, B, C, D, F letter-grade system
- the 1–5 point-scale system
- the + ✓ − system
- your own rating system

Whatever system you use, **be sure to explain the score you've given and to include specific examples from the text to support the score** so that Professor L. will understand your assessment.

Task Postcard # 003-91

CRITIQUE THE CHAPTER

Write a postcard to Professor Ron L., head author of your math textbook *Middle School Math, Course 3*, telling him **your opinion** of Chapter 2, Integer Operations.

Critique the chapter, telling what worked well for you in learning about adding, subtracting, multiplying, and dividing integers and what did not work well. Share both your positive and negative opinions of the chapter. (For example, maybe you liked the practice exercises because they helped you "get it," but the pages were too crowded for your eyes.)

Be honest in your feedback, and be sure to **include specific examples** from the chapter to support the opinion you give Professor L.

Task Postcard # ZT-40

IMPROVE THE CHAPTER

Write a postcard to Professor Ron L., head author of your math textbook *Middle School Math, Course 3*, telling him **how to improve** Chapter 2, Integer Operations.

Point out to him and his three coauthors what they could have done differently in the chapter to make it a better tool for teaching you how to add, subtract, multiply, and divide integers.

Be helpful in your suggestions so that the authors will be inclined to take your advice in improving the chapter for other middle school math students.

Be specific in your recommendations. Keep in mind that comments like "Make it more fun" or "Make it more interesting" are too vague to be helpful.

Please notice the following about the leveled assignment:

- All three task cards deal with the same topic: feedback to the author.
- All three task cards require students to evaluate the effectiveness of a chapter from their math textbook: Critical analysis is the common objective.
- All three task cards look similar: They share the same format.
- All three task cards offer some examples on how to proceed: There's no reason to intentionally commit "assumicide" by giving students an unclear assignment.
- All three task cards are challenging, respectful, and novel: The goal is gaining and maintaining student interest in learning about integers.
- The task cards are tiered by level of difficulty.

- The levels of difficulty are disguised: Rather than numbering them Level 1, 2, and 3, I used random letter/number combinations. I find that this tends to prevent resistance to any level. (Some teachers, however, prefer to be upfront with the tiers and label from least to most challenging.)

Now the big question: How can a teacher organize his or her instructional plans around these three levels to support students' development as careful, thoughtful, critical readers of their beloved math textbook? Four options are outlined in the chart on pages 58–59.

> For guidance on creating cooperative groups in literature, I recommend *Literature Circles: Voice and Choice in Book Clubs and Reading Groups*, by Harvey Daniels (Stenhouse, 2001). You'll also find many ideas for multipurpose grouping in *Designing Group Work: Strategies for the Heterogeneous Classroom* by Elizabeth G. Cohen (Teachers College Press, 1994).

Nudging Our Students Forward

Whether we are teaching literature or science, fiction or informational text, all of us are interested in helping students improve their critical-thinking skills. Unfortunately, providing a motivating purpose and an authentic audience is sometimes not enough. Let's examine some teaching techniques that will advance their reading-writing analysis skills to help move them beyond a typical basic-level response.

DEVELOPING TIERED LEVELS

First, we can appropriately challenge students by designing tiered assignments. We explored this technique earlier with the example of the leveled response tasks created for students reviewing a math textbook chapter on integers. In that example, the three tiered tasks are aligned with the three levels of the taxonomy I recommended earlier for textbook feedback: rating, critiquing, and improving.

Create the Assignments

Tiered levels can be designed by beginning with a solid "baseline" assignment—an assignment that provides a starting point from which you can increase or decrease the level of difficulty. You might want to revisit an assignment you've had success with in the past or try out a brand new one. In either case, plan ahead for student differences. For an assignment you've used before, remember the pitfalls that some students experienced: unclear directions, difficult concepts or parts of the task, or missing steps. Likewise, think about elements that held back other students: tasks or concepts that were too easy, redundant information, or parts that seemed trivial to them. For a new assignment, anticipate elements that some students will find too easy or too hard.

Based on the first trial of an assignment, you can retool the assignment into tiers of difficulty, or challenge levels, as Diane Heacox calls them in her book *Differentiating*

Instruction in the Regular Classroom. I like to design three levels, or tiers, for an assignment.

1. Basic (the task meets the bottom-line learning objective)

2. More Challenging

3. Advanced

I take the original baseline assignment and rework it to create a Tier 2 assignment. I clarify the directions and add some steps. I then work backward, reducing or scaffolding some elements to create a less-complex Tier 1 assignment. To develop a Tier 3 assignment I build onto the Tier 2 assignment, increasing the challenge. You may want to refer to the list of verbs below to help you plan tiered activities.

> Consider the language that best reflects your goals and meets the needs of your students. Middle-school teacher and author Rick Wormeli uses the following labels for himself when he designs tiered tasks: "grade level," "advanced level," and "early readiness level" (2006).

Levels-of-Thinking Verbs

Using precise language when you plan your lessons or phrase questions can help you target all levels of thinking.

Knowledge	Comprehension	Application	Analysis	Synthesis	Evaluation
Memorize	Explain	Show	Survey	Design	Defend
Define	Predict	Illustrate	Compare or Contrast	Rewrite	Choose
Label	Summarize	Sequence	Examine	Construct	Prioritize

From *Learning to Teach* © 2005 by Linda Shalaway

Keep in mind that all three tiers must be interesting, challenging, and meet or exceed your grade-level standards. In other words, a Tier 1 assignment cannot be so simplistic that the concepts you want the class to grasp are lost or so easy that it serves only as a time-filler, while assignments at Tiers 2 and 3 are challenging, interesting, and fun. Finally, as I suggested earlier, be sensitive to students when you label the assignments.

Match Students to the Assignments

After you've designed the tiered assignments, use what you know about students' background knowledge, aptitudes, interests, and energy levels to select the assignment that's best suited for each student. Of course, another option is to let students select the tier they want to try. Student choice is another element of differentiated instruction, and it has definite benefits as well as some drawbacks. (See troubleshooting tip 3 on page 59.)

Planning Tiered Lessons for Response Writing

Assignment Option 1

Assign all students to write the Level 1 assignment as an introduction to this type of response writing. (This is particularly helpful when the entire class is unfamiliar with writing a critical response to literature.)

Tip

Assigning every student the basic Level 1 task, such as a response postcard rating a textbook chapter, is okay. We're in no rush here. Later, after the class has studied another chapter of the textbook, you may want to assign a Level 2 task to every student with the clearly stated objective of sharpening their critical thinking and improving the quality of their responses. Several weeks or a month later, when the class has advanced further in the text, assign the Level 3 task and tell the class that they're all progressing in their ability to analyze informational texts.

Assignment Option 2

Assign different levels to different students based on their individual skills and current abilities. That is, those students who are struggling with the reading or with responding could be assigned the Level 1 task, those who are reading well and able to write decently take the Level 2 task, and those who need more challenge can attempt the Level 3 task. This approach ensures success in learning for all.

Tip

How do you know you've appropriately matched students to the leveled assignments when their current math skill level, for example, may not accurately reflect their critical reading and writing skills? So long as you always accommodate students when you see them struggle with or breeze through an assignment, you're on track. It's part of ongoing assessment; we know that students' abilities can change, and we know that our evaluation of their abilities can change. If we assign a task that's too easy or too hard, we identify the problem and make adjustments. No harm, no foul.

Assignment Option 3

Allow students to choose which postcard they want to write. Student choice is a recommended practice of differentiated instruction. Letting students pick which assignment they are interested in doing is a nice change of pace once in a while. They appreciate having some input in and ownership of their educational experience.

Planning Tiered Lessons for Response Writing

Tip

You may encounter resistance from unmotivated students who choose to do the minimum amount or least challenging work required. You can urge them to a more appropriate level by using these techniques:

- disguising the levels of the tiered tasks, as I did with the math cards above, and handing them the one that best meets their needs

- offering an incentive to "choose up" by awarding more points to students who complete more challenging levels

- looking the kid in the eye and saying, "I think you can handle Level 3, and because I want you to succeed at it, I promise to come by your desk three times this period to help you in any way you need it. Anything you need to get started? Okay, I'll be back in four minutes and 22 seconds. Let's see how much you can do on your own."

Assignment Option 4

Turn this writing assignment into a cooperative writing activity with students working in pairs or trios to draft their response writing. This option mitigates the frustration some students may feel if the assignment is too challenging for them to complete alone; they now have built-in support from a classmate. This is cooperative learning: teaming students when they're not yet ready to go solo.

Tip

You will want to avoid group work situations in which only one student does the work while the others are off-task. Well-planned cooperative learning assignments build in key ingredients for success so that all group members participate in and learn from the assignment. First, set ground rules for individual accountability as well as group/team work. For example, before the partners get together to write a Level 2 or 3 postcard, have each student write a first draft independently. That way, when they join as a pair or trio, they begin by putting their solo attempts on the table for the partner's consideration. Partners can pick the best parts from both of their drafts to create their improved cowritten version. Second, give clear directions and expectations for how you want students to participate in the group, handle disagreements, and manage their time. Tell them up front.

You may find it helpful to form temporary small groups based on tiers. For example, you might call all students working on the Tier 1 assignment together for an orientation session in order to further describe the assignment's purpose, to debug any difficult directions, to answer students' questions, and generally motivate students and get them headed in the right direction.

Assess and Adjust

Remember that your ultimate goal is to help all students reach increasingly higher levels of critical thinking and comprehension. Therefore, watch students and ask yourself whether the assignment they are working on is demanding, meaningful, interesting, respectful of their abilities, and at or above grade-level standards. And students assigned Tier 1 or 2 tasks should be given the opportunity to try working at a Tier 2 or 3 task as soon as they are ready. We want to continuously nudge each and every learner forward.

PROVIDING PROMPTS AND CLARIFYING EXPECTATIONS

In all the response assignment examples I've presented so far, students are given a clear prompt, that is, a clear purpose, audience, and topic to write about. We owe it to students to provide as much helpful structure as possible to support their success in the demanding venture known as "writing." This is especially true when we ask students to write in a new genre, like critical-response writing. (An exception would be a creative-response assignment in which you may want to leave more decisions about shaping the response to the students. But for meeting the needs of the most reluctant writers with little experience writing in this genre, I strongly advocate for clarity of purpose, audience, topic, and structure in advance to help these writers succeed.)

Another vehicle for success is to describe the assessment tool you're using with the assignment. Students not only perform better with a clear prompt to guide them, but also with a solid understanding of how their work will be evaluated. That's why I have recommended designing, distributing, and discussing student-friendly assessment tools like ChecBrics (see Chapter 4). Ultimately, you'll want to select something that works for both you and your students.

MODELING WITH STUDENT-RESPONSE SAMPLES

Showing students models of a student-written response assignment goes even further in assisting their writing process and their understanding of the task. While rubrics or, better yet, ChecBrics serve to guide students as they write by highlighting critically important components of an assignment, an actual written response to that assignment demonstrates how another writer processed the prompt, organized their ideas, and phrased their response: Through examples, students see the *real* thing.

When you model with student work, make sure you have samples that reflect various degrees of success on an assignment. In fact, I think the best example for students is to see a response that is partially successful, but falls short in some areas. A constant diet of high-quality student samples can be discouraging to some students. I lead a discussion on what worked, what did not, and how we could do better. That's the key: What we could *do better* on our own attempts.

Also, I lead the class in employing the ChecBric to score the samples. We discuss what *specifically* worked, what did not work, and what areas (traits/targets) met the basic requirements, but surely could be improved by "doing something else." The something else, of course, comes from quoting the elements defined in the ChecBric. This procedure gives students a clear indication of not only what they are supposed to do on the assignment, but also how they can expect to be assessed on the assignment.

Another useful teaching technique to use when you model with students' writing is to assign students to rewrite the sample paper "upwards"—that is, to revise someone else's attempt and improve upon it by following the guidelines of the assignment.

> ### Make a Habit of Saving Student Work
>
> As the saying goes, "A picture is worth a thousand words." I collect a set of "pictures" from each task I assign to share with other classes the next time I assign the same task. These samples range in quality so I have examples from basic to exceptional. Be mindful of students' privacy, and always ask a student's permission to use his or her paper as a model, and remove his or her name when you copy the writing.

MODELING THE WRITING PROCESS

Just as sharing student-written models is an effective way to show what a completed assignment looks like, composing the assignment on the board or overhead as students observe is an effective way to show how to follow the assignment directions and put ideas onto paper in an organized way. Teacher modeling is the master-apprentice model.

Alfie Kohn describes this approach as *deep modeling*—taking students backstage to let them in on the practices experts use:

> Deep modeling might be thought of as a way of taking children "backstage." To that extent, it's very much like writing—or conducting an authentic science experiment—in front of them. They're able to experience what happens before (or behind or beneath) the ethical decisions that adults make, the essays they publish, and the scientific principles they discover—all of which are usually presented to children as so many *faits accomplis*.

> This has several advantages, the most obvious of which is that experiencing the process helps them to become more proficient. . . . Students should have the chance to watch their teachers write so these students will learn more about, and get better at, the craft of writing. By the same token, children presumably would become more skillful at solving math problems, or make better moral decisions, as a result of seeing how adults do those things (2006).

Kohn writes about improving students' disposition to emulate what the teacher does. This is important: affecting our students' *disposition* to write at more advanced levels of critique and analysis.

Even if we feel that we are not "masters" of the craft of writing, it is still very helpful for our students to observe us wrestling with the assignment and, at times, asking for student input. It reveals to them that writing is a challenge, but it can be done by making thoughtful decisions at varying points in the process. And even if the results of our writing are not as successful as we would expect, we now have created a sample paper on the assignment—to return to, critique, and improve.

When you model writing for students, aim to make your process transparent by thinking aloud—comment especially on the elements you most want students to include in their writing, such as addressing the author in a respectful tone of voice. Comment on your awareness of your audience's potential reaction to the way you've phrased criticisms; show your desire to avoid offending the author with comments that offer friendly advice and provide support rather than seeming haughty, irritated, grouchy, or grumpy.

✛✛✛✛✛✛✛✛✛✛✛✛✛✛✛✛✛✛ Reality Check ✛✛✛✛✛✛✛✛✛✛✛✛✛✛✛✛✛✛

While I have found that student-to-author talk-back writing assignments in tandem with reading nonfiction are the most motivating I have ever used, they have not caused every last student to abandon their cares and dance lightly through the task of writing to the textbook author. Even the novelty of the assignment and its potential to empower students, even with lots of student and teacher modeling, and even with a cool ChecBric to keep them on track, critical-response writing can still be a tough task, and students find this out when they make their first attempt to compose a memo, postcard, or letter to the author.

This is okay, I tell them and myself. Tough is good. We are moving them forward, perhaps slower than we would like, but forward nonetheless. And I know—and reassure students—that with practice, response writing gets easier over the course of the semester or school year.

One More Structure: The Proposal Letter

It's clear that students can use postcards and memos to critique the nonfiction reading assignments we give them, just as they can with fiction response assignments. Can we push them further still to write effective response letters? Absolutely.

In Chapter 1 we considered using the friendly letter as the third writing structure for student feedback to authors of fiction. With nonfiction response assignments, I recommend we teach students to develop study-aid materials, such as a study guide for a chapter, and write a cover letter that presents the guide to the author or publisher.

PHYSICAL SCIENCE CHAPTER STUDY GUIDE AND COVER LETTER: AN EXAMPLE

Olivia, a ninth grader in Jud Landis' Physical Science course at Sheldon High School in Eugene, Oregon, composed her own version of Chapter 3 of the physical science textbook. Titled "Chapter 3 Study Guide," Olivia's writing offers a synopsis of the chapter's nine boldfaced sections and includes formulas, illustrations, and a glossary of key terms used in the chapter (for more images, see page 111).

> Teacher, author, and idea hatcher Jim Burke describes an innovative reading-writing assignment in his book *Reading Reminders*. He decided that his English students at Burlingame High School in California would better comprehend and appreciate the literature selections he assigned if they had to compose their own version of a CliffsNotes™ guide. I'll explain in detail how to teach this advanced response-writing in Chapter 6.

Chapter 3 Study Guide

By: Olivia

Including a whole list of important vocab! from the chapter! (in the BACK)

The student-written study guide assignment has multiple audiences, which makes it a meaningful assignment for students. In this example, Olivia writes first for herself in order to learn and retain the material. Second, she shares her booklet with her classmates in a review activity. A third audience is the teacher and future classes of students. Jud Landis deputized the class to assist him in planning for the same course next semester; he told Olivia and her classmates that he would share guides they had created with his new class. Finally, the audience may include the book's author or publisher.

To help Olivia extend her audience for her thoughtful guide, I asked her to write a proposal letter to the publisher offering her student-authored study guide to the company as a possible supplemental resource. We then discussed writing to the author first in an attempt to get his opinion with hopes that he would like her study guide and see its value for other students using his text. We figured he could become an important ally in convincing the publishing company to go for her proposal. So she e-mailed a letter to him with the address I found on his Web site.

Dear Mr. H___,

I have an unusual request for you. I would like you to consider publishing a study guide booklet I created last term in my ninth grade physical science class for a section in your science textbook *Conceptual Physics*.

It was actually an assignment everyone in my class was required to do by my teacher, Jud Landis, Sheldon High School, in Eugene, Oregon, and I think that it was a good idea because I learned the material better by creating this study guide. The study guide I made has pictures in it, which also helped me learn the material better.

Like you, I enjoy drawing, and it adds to my writing, don't you think?

In making this study guide, it helped me to memorize the material much easier than just from my science book, and having the pictures in the study guide made it much more fun and interesting. Also, since I did this study guide, my teacher got to check if I, and the other students, understood the material. My teacher is going to use these study guides created by students in my class for students in the upcoming years. These students will definitely benefit from these study guides, and I think if your publisher publishes my study guide, many other kids could benefit from it too! Anyone who needs to learn the lessons from that science section from the textbook would be much more successful in understanding it! You know, a kid-to-kid version of the concepts.

The idea of sending you a copy for your consideration came from another teacher who worked with my teacher and gave him the study-guide idea. He thought my guide was one of the best in the whole class.

I hope you consider my offer to you and publish my study guide! Please look it over and let me know what you think.

Thanks very much.

Sincerely,

Olivia

The benefits of this reading-writing assignment are obvious. The student has elevated her status from ninth-grade science student to the author of a resource. Her audience is a real one—a respected academic in the field of physics. And I'll bet that Olivia will forever know that textbook authors are not mystical deities, but people who communicate useful information to an audience. Just like she did.

Here is the reply she received from the author, who found her proposal worthy of a response:

> Hello Olivia,
>
> Thank you for sharing your Chapter 3 study guide with me. I am honored. Although such wouldn't meet the requirements of my publisher for publication, I see it as a great resource to share with others in your school. And in time, it's a safe bet that it is an important stepping-stone in your personal and professional development. You have the quality important for good writing—being able to get to the crux of a thing, sidestepping less important material. I commend you for your very talented effort!

Though the proposal was not accepted—and we had discussed that this might be a longshot—Olivia received the kind of feedback and encouragement from the author that makes the assignment so worth the effort. In fact, she decided to try again by sending a proposal letter directly to the publishing company, the results of which you can find in Chapter 6.

COACHING TIPS FOR PROPOSAL LETTER–WRITING

To help them write a good proposal letter, tell students to do these things:

1. Reveal the context:
Tell the company where you go to school, what class/course you are in, who is your teacher, and what topic you were studying. (Note: Check your school's confidentiality policy to determine how much background information students are permitted to share in this situation.)

2. Explain the purpose(s):
Tell the company what you are trying to accomplish and why.

3. Tell the company the possible benefits of publishing your study guide booklet; "sell" them on the idea.

4. Be courteous:
As with all talk-back assignments, the recipient/audience likely will be surprised, and may even be taken aback, so when presenting your proposal, be honest, but also be polite; come across as an ally, a friend of the company.

PUTTING YOUR BEST FOOT FORWARD: EDITING THE PROPOSAL LETTERS

Before you mail students' proposal letters to the textbook's publisher, you'll want students to make sure they have put their best foot forward; that is, they must maximize their chances for success by sending the very best proposal letter to accompany the very best booklet they can produce. So, they will need to edit them well.

Just like postcards, memos, or Dear Author letters, when proposal letters leave the protected environment of the classroom and enter the real world, students must understand how readers react to mistakes. This is the time to explain the impact that mistakes, including misspelled words, misuse of punctuation, sloppiness, confusing paragraphs, unsupported ideas, sentence fragments, and trite, overused vocabulary have on the reading audience. To prove it, hand out a worksheet with typos, confusing directions, or improper grammar. This is the perfect moment to talk about *considerate writers* and what they do to help their readers understand and appreciate what they've done.

Tell the class, "By the way, this is called editing, and it means that you have *another chance* to consider the effect your writing will have on your audience."

Another chance—that's a whole lot better than perceiving this stage of the writing process to be a teacher-mandated punishment. Getting students to revisit and improve their writing will take some work on our part because many students really do think that revision is a burden to be avoided at all costs. We must turn it around so they begin to view it as a writer's right, to see it as a good deal that the first draft doesn't have to go out with its half-baked ideas, its tentative sentences, its guess-and-go spellings.

Questioning authority. Not a desired form of communication in most schools. But in the context of this chapter, it means the student-reader becomes a writer who gives honest, analytical, supported feedback to an authority, the professional writer, who in turn becomes the audience. Nice role reversal.

To pull this off, we considered the same writing structures for addressing nonfiction reading assignments as we did for fiction reading assignments. As in Chapter 1, I described prompts, writing structures, scoring devices, and teaching tips to help make this a successful teaching experience for you and a rewarding writing experience for your students. Additionally, this chapter offered ways to meet the needs of each student with response assignments through differentiated instruction techniques, including tiered assignments and temporary grouping.

We finished with reality rearing its ugly head: Before any student-to-author communication gets sent out of the classroom, editing must be done. Because students often view this activity as a laborious exercise, we must address it in detail, as well as the logistical issues of contacting authors, so that the edited, polished student work can be mailed.

These are big issues, so let's address revision strategies in Chapter 3.

RE-VISION: BECOMING A CONSIDERATE WRITER

The beautiful part of writing is that you don't have to get it right the first time, unlike, say, a brain surgeon. You can always do it better. . . .

—Robert Cormier

In this rough-draft student-to-author postcard about one of my stories, an eighth grader uses the Praise-Question-Polish (P-Q-P) response format I introduced in Chapter 1.

> Dear Leon,
>
> I like how your story starts out because the buyer says that you should not forget my two fifty dollar bills so he can negotiate with the seller.
>
> My biggest question is why didn't you name the characters. Was it because you wanted to make the story more interesting or confusing?
>
> I thought your story was really good, but one thing I would do to make the story easier to read is give the characters names because I never read story characters without any names before.
>
> Sincerely,
>
> Lance
>
> Best Wishes

My initial reaction to Lance's criticism of the story is one of congratulations. I wrote, *Nice job, Lance, for using the P-Q-P format to structure your feedback postcard. You covered all three areas, and you organized them into three distinct paragraphs to make it easy for me to read.*

Indeed, Lance's postcard is a rough draft, an initial attempt to deliver his reactions to the story back to the author. And because it is a first draft, the author should never see it. (In this case, I happened to be the author and the teacher, so I read the response early in its development.) For a first attempt, a positive response is fine.

When students are ready to go further in their responses, and especially if you plan to send their responses to the author, it's time to teach them to revise their writing. The revision strategies described in this chapter help you and your students arrive at a polished response—writing that everyone feels good about sending to the author. Ultimately the goal of the revision approach I present is to train students to expect more from their writing and to appreciate having time to review what they wrote and make improvements—to re-envision their response.

The Challenge of Writing: Seeing Revision as an Opportunity

Writing is a demanding venture, as any writer will readily admit. From professionally published authors to college professors and graduate students, from reporters to office workers, from school teachers to their students, everyone knows how tough it can be to write.

Here's the challenge: Writing requires the transfer of ideas residing in the mind to specific words onto paper, words that must fit into sentences that flow nicely, sentences that unite to form paragraphs that build upon each other to organize the thoughts. The words need to be the best ones available to capture the thoughts, and they must be spelled in a standard way. Sentences need subjects and predicates that work together, and they need capital letters and punctuation marks that are set in the proper places. The tone of voice must match the topic and sound authentic, true, and engaging. In other words, the creator of all this, whom we call the writer, has dozens of choices to make in the transfer of ideas from the head to the paper. And each choice has an impact on the reader.

An impact on the reader. This is what writing is all about. Without the reader, there is no writing. Without the audience, there is no purpose. Even in reflective writing where the writer writes privately for him- or herself, the reader is everything to a writer, supplying motivation for the writer to communicate clearly and to affect the reader with his or her words.

The problem is, too many of our students do not think about the reader. Instead, they think about the parameters of the task: *How long must this writing assignment be? When it is due? What effect will the grade have on the final grade?* And they may spend quite a lot of brainpower figuring out how to do as little work as possible and still get a decent grade. Not all students think like this, but I believe many of them do. They don't write like a reader; they write like a victim.

If students view writing as something assigned in school to and for the teacher, then they won't write as though they're communicating important ideas to someone who needs to receive them. And if students want to get through writing as painlessly as possible or avoid it all together, then they won't see revision as an opportunity; they'll take it as a cruel teacher-inflicted punishment.

Here are some ideas about ways to overcome this attitude and teach our students to envision the process like real writers. We want them to understand Richard North Patterson's notion that "writing *is* rewriting . . ." and take Justice Louis Brandeis's advice: "There is no great writing, only great rewriting."

> **Revision** = to see again
>
> **Revision** ≠ a punishment

BECOMING A CONSIDERATE WRITER

In Chapter 2, I suggested that student-to-author writing is the perfect opportunity to reteach our students about revision. Because they have a real reason to write and a real audience to address, their writing is a communication rather than merely an assignment, and therefore, it is important enough to be the best it can possibly be. Writing to an author makes the act of rewriting far more concrete than rewriting for a teacher.

Tell your students, "You have worked hard to gather your thoughts about this reading assignment and send them down your arm out onto the paper. You have made many decisions about how to express those thoughts. Each decision you've made should have been to help your audience, the author, understand exactly what you thought about the writing. Each word you chose, each sentence you wrote, each paragraph you built was intended to welcome the author into your mind, so that a conversation about the writing could occur.

"And I have good news for you: Before we send your work to the author, you have the chance to tidy up your writing, to rethink it, to improve it, to make it match the ideas in your head as closely as possible. You want to be *considerate* of the author, so that he [or she] has the very best chance of understanding your opinions, your questions, your suggestions. Treat the author well. Be a *courteous* writer." And I remind them of Cormier's notion that writers, unlike brain surgeons, "don't have to get it right the first time"—in fact they can "always do it better."

Most importantly, assure them that they will receive help doing it better—lots of help. And I guide them through a three-stage revision process.

Three Rounds of Repair

Because writing is actually rewriting (and rewriting some more), we must teach our students why, when, and how to rewrite.

I recommend we teach this in three rounds of *repair*. I use the term *repair* for rewriting because it fits into a four-stage writing process I offer students who have not yet developed their own process for writing. I call these stages Prepare, First Dare, Repair, and Share. They are aligned with the writing process stages commonly referred to as prewriting, drafting, revision and editing, and publishing. I prefer my labels because the language appeals to the middle schoolers with whom I work and because they're easy to remember: They rhyme.

In my book *Paving the Way in Reading and Writing* (Jossey Bass, 2003), you can read more about the four writing-process stages I use in my instruction.

The Repair stage provides three opportunities, or three *rounds*, to "repair their first dare" (edit their first draft):

1. Self-Editing

2. Peer Editing

3. Teacher-Student Editing Conference

The trick, of course, is to structure each round in an engaging, meaningful way, so that students will see the benefits of this work and be willing to try.

ROUND 1: SELF-EDITING

To cultivate in students a sense of ownership and control over their work, have students begin the revision stage of the writing process independently. Instruct students to "self-repair" for Round 1 (assure them that in Round 2 they will be paired or grouped). We want them to have the same experience a professional writer has when writing for publication: the opportunity to be the first to consider the draft before exposing it to someone else. That way, the writer can tune it up and move it closer to his or her vision before someone else gets a crack at it.

Of course, students will need some assistance in this venture. Self-editing comes as a major role-reversal for students: First they were the writers, the authors, who by definition, are close to their writing. Now, they are expected to distance themselves from that hard-earned writing and take on the role of editor—a detached, critical observer of the writing.

Here are some simple self-editing strategies to try with your students:

Oral Reading

We often assign students to silently reread their drafts and are surprised when they turn up nothing in an error-riddled paper—why is this? When a writer silently rereads a draft, he or she is reading familiar material at a rapid rate and frequently substituting words that were intended but never ended up on the paper—or otherwise fixing errors—and moving on. In contrast, soft oral reading slows down the rereading process and highlights errors by sound, allowing the writer to hear what he or she wrote, word for word.

Several techniques can assist students with oral reading for revision. First, I use an idea I learned in one of my workshops from Arizona teacher Leslie Green: Provide student-editors with a colored pencil to contrast with the graphite pencil they used to write the draft. As they quietly reread, encourage them to "use the colored pencil to show where the pencil you used to write your draft was not able to keep up with your brain;" if they find a point of confusion or an error, they must make the change in color. I like this technique very much because it puts the responsibility for any deficiency in the draft on the pencil, not on a student's brain. While it does not enable every student to spot every glitch that needs fixing, reading quietly with the colored pencil usually helps students catch some of the shortcomings in their drafts.

Two other techniques can help to keep the rereading at a manageable noise level so students can hear themselves read. One is to provide self-editors with a "telephone" to read into. Constructed with a 6- to 9-inch piece of PVC plumber's white plastic pipe with U-shaped couplers attached to both ends, this device allows a student to whisper-read into the mouthpiece and hear it clearly in the earpiece. It not only keeps the noise level down for neighbors, students really enjoy using it—I've been told it's a "cool" writing tool.

Similarly, students may use the "earmuff" technique while self-editing. They cover their ears with their hands as they very softly read their drafts. The sound reverberates in their cranium while they simultaneously block out other noises in the environment. Try it—it works. The upside is it requires only students' own hands, but the downside is that both of their hands are occupied, so they can't simultaneously use the colored pencil to make changes. But they can drop their hands from their ears occasionally to edit.

> Why are first drafts so full of errors? The problem for young writers (really, for all writers) is that the flow of thoughts from the brain to the paper easily gets scrambled. As literacy expert Linda Christensen notes, it is exceedingly difficult to "match the paper in my mind to one I am writing down" (2000). We simply cannot write as fast as we can think (we can't even type as fast as we think) and this causes us to write imperfect drafts.

> Have students skip lines on their drafts to allow themselves plenty of room for making changes.

The Editor's Table

This special workstation helps students transition from writer to editor. After finishing a draft, students move from their desks to the Editor's Table to physically reinforce the major role-reversal described above.

The Editor's Table is merely a table off to the side or in the back of the classroom that has four chairs and is equipped with editing tools: colored pens and pencils, highlighters, sticky-notes, correction fluid or white tape, erasers, tape, dictionaries, thesauruses, and a spelling dictionary.

Why only four chairs at the table? More than four encourages conversation, and the only talking allowed here is self-talking. You can assure them that they will be able to talk about their draft with a classmate, but that will occur later, in Round 2.

As you adapt this strategy to meet the needs of you and your students, consider room space and logistics. What if your classroom doesn't have the space to set up a table? Some classrooms are jam-packed with student desks. A few alternatives to consider include setting up the Editor's Table in the hallway, setting up your desk as the temporary Editor's Table, or letting students who are ready to revise transform their own desk into the Editor's Table with a portable Editor's Box (a shoebox filled with some of the tools listed above).

Be sure to work out the logistical issues before you invite students to work at the table. Consider how this technique can be structured to avoid off-task behaviors and to promote productivity. I suggest creating a set of class rules for Editing Time that you discuss with the class and enforce consistently. For example, you might require them to sign up on the board for a chair at the table and take their turn in the order they've signed up, so no mad rush occurs when a chair becomes available. Also, consider rules for what students are to do between the time they finish their draft and a seat at the table is available, how much time students get at the table, and how you expect them to function independently and respectfully. If you'd like to view my List of Rules, check them out at my Web site http://www.larrylewin.com/books.

The Sentence Opening Sheet

This is my favorite self-editing technique. Invented by Bob Cahill and Herb Hrebic of the Stack the Deck Writing Program, it is designed to get students to independently re-see their draft with fresh eyes.

The amazing thing to me is that most kids never think about revision as *re-vision*. *Revision* means *to see again*. To help student really see what they did in their drafts, the Sentence Opening Sheet (SOS) guides them through a reformatting exercise in four parts. They answer each part in a column on the sheet:

Column 1: Sentence openers (Students assess whether there is variety or redundancy in the way they begin sentences.)

Column 2: Special (In this open column the teacher focuses on any pet peeve in student writing that needs adjustment.)

Column 3: Verbs (Students determine whether they have used mostly active or passive voice, observed proper subject-verb agreement, stayed consistent in the tense, and chosen trite or bright verbs.)

Column 4: Total number of words per sentence (Students compare the length and fluency of the sentences they've written.)

In the sample Sentence Opening Sheet below, Joshua discovers that several sentence openings are repetitive and that sentences 2–5 are all about the same length. He comments on both issues in his reflection at the bottom of the page. Notice that column 2 is blank—the teacher decided not to add the special challenge for this round of revision.

There are several teaching tips to consider when using this self-editing technique:

1. Since students will need to transcribe their sentence openings onto the worksheet, have them number each sentence in their draft (writing "#1" in front of the first sentence, "#2" in front of the second, and so on) before they begin this revision work.

2. Build slowly instead of overwhelming students with instructions. I suggest you teach students how to do columns 1 and 4 the first time. In another lesson, you can introduce the other columns.

3. Once you have trained your class to answer the prompts in all four columns, make plenty of copies of the Sentence Opening Sheet (page 75) and have them available for students to pick up when they finish their drafts. The goal is to facilitate independent self-editing—students may pick up an S.O.S. on their way to the Editor's Table or they may chose to do the S.O.S. at their desks while waiting their turn.

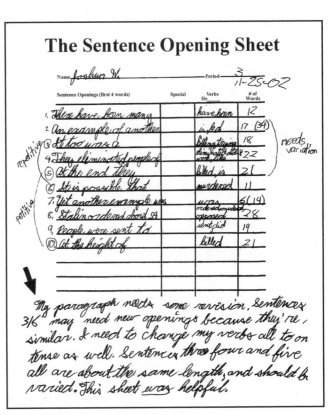

4. If students' drafts are very long, say three or more pages, tell them to use the S.O.S. for the first page only or to analyze six selected paragraphs. (Let's not turn this activity into a punishment by overdoing it.)

5. Instruct students to write a summary self-reflective statement at the bottom of their S.O.S. indicating what their self-analysis revealed about their draft. You might also require them to make a commitment to change their draft in some way(s) based on their S.O.S. analysis.

Visit the Stack the Deck Web site at http://www.stack thedeck.com/tips-great.html to learn more about their Sentence Opening Sheet technique and to see how teachers have modified it to better assist their students.

6. Use the S.O.S. as a bridge from Round 1 to Round 2. Even though it was designed for independent self-editing, you may want to have students hand their completed sheet over to the peer editor in Round 2 so that the new editor can evaluate how well the revision is going.

Motivating Students for Revision

For students who may stall out on the energy required for self-editing or peer editing, I recommend getting a large envelope, addressing it to the author, and affixing postage to it. Bring it to class and carry it around the room as you check in with your students. I either hold it in my hand or set it on a student's desk depending on how much of an impact I need to make. Typically, when students see the actual envelope, the reality of the assignment gives them a major jolt. I've had students look at the envelope, pause, and then ask me in disbelief, "You're really gonna send my work to the author?" I reply, "Yep. Is it ready to go in the envelope, or do you need more time revising it?" And then, "Do you need some help to get it ready to go?"

ROUND 2: PEER EDITING

After students have had the opportunity to rework their drafts on their own, it's time for a "little help from their friends."

Round 2 is Peer Editing, and many, many of us have incorporated this technique into our teaching of writing. And many, many of us have mixed feelings about the results. I'm pretty sure I used Peer Editing in every year of my teaching career, and I am very sure that it rarely went as well as I had intended.

Why is peer review so prone to disappointment? Why is it so difficult to pull off successfully? I believe it is because the role of editor is a very demanding job. My friend, author and artist Tom Bamberger, hit it right on the head when he described

Name _____ Date _____

Sentence Opening Sheet

First Four Words Per Sentence	Special	Verbs	Number of Words

What I discovered about my draft:

what his editor did for him: "She is a very careful reader." That's exactly right. A good editor is a good reader, a careful *pre*reader who is on the lookout for potentially tricky places that could disrupt the reading audience's understanding of the writer's intended message. They have the tough job of working at the interface of writer and reader— and good editors help to make that connection as strong as it can be.

To help students assume this role and play it well, let's provide them with structured support for peer editing. Here are three teaching tips to add to your repertoire:

1. **Intensify the role.** Tell students that the partner who is editing must role-play the actual audience. That is, the peer editor will assume the persona of the author who will be eventually receiving this written feedback. I even suggest having the student-editor introduce him- or herself as Gary Soto, Katherine Patterson, William Shakespeare, or whomever the author is, and shake hands with the student-writer. This approach should remind both writer and editor who the audience is on this assignment and motivate the peer editor to take this job seriously. The editor's job is to imagine how the author might react to the student-writer's feedback and to seek clarification on the draft, so that he or she can optimally understand the student-writer's opinions. Encourage students to stay focused on this job and not to get carried away with the role play—We don't want them to go overboard and debate their partner in an attempt to defend the work against a critique. Rather, we want them to be a "mine sweeper" and alert the writer to any potential problems that the reader could have.

> To help student-editors "get into character" to role-play the author, give them some question-starter prompts that seek clarification from the student-writer:
>
> "What do you mean by _____?"
>
> "Are you saying that _____?"
>
> "Do you think that _____?"
>
> "Why do you suggest that _____?"
>
> "When did you come up with _____?"

2. **Narrow the focus.** Highly skilled editors can handle multiple issues simultaneously. They read drafts and troubleshoot content issues, usage issues, organizational issues, vocabulary issues, and on and on. Novice editors like our students can handle fewer issues. We know this, so let's give them a limited amount on their radar. How many issues are reasonable? I find that three editing tasks are usually plenty. Education writer John Collins agrees. In his "Focused Correction Areas" approach, he recommends that teachers select three targets for review and make sure student writers and editors know which three are targeted before they begin their drafting (2006). To this end, you may want to use a Partner Checklist to itemize the targeted

areas that the peer editor will be required to address. I do the same, but I bring in the ChecBric instead of a Checklist. (See Round 3.)

3. **Mix and match:** Whether you prefer students working in pairs, trios, or in groups of four or five, the decision regarding who works with whom looms over this technique. Is it better for the teacher to assign partners or to let the kids select their own partners? Both options have obvious benefits as well as obvious drawbacks. Let me suggest a compromise I learned from Allyne Lawson, an art teacher at Chatsworth High School in California who discovered the idea in Donna Kay Beattie's *Assessment in Art Education* (1997). Beattie suggests allowing students two response partners, one assigned by the teacher (who often knows best) and the other selected by the student (who believes he or she knows best). Beattie designed it for peer review of art, but Allyne saw that it transferred easily to peer review of writing. She designed a peer response sheet that's simple to create and provides space for comments from both reviewers. The writer attaches his or her draft in the center of an 11- by 17-inch piece of paper to create a "flap" for reviewer response on either side. Each peer reviewer writes comments about the draft on one flap. The flaps can be folded over to keep the comments private.

Peer Editing—A Compromise

Student chooses **Peer Reviewer #1**		Teacher assigns **Peer Reviewer #2**
Reviewer reads draft and responds to a set of prompts:		Reviewer reads draft and responds to a set of prompts:
1.	Student affixes draft in center	1.
2.		2.
3.		3.
fold flap over →		← fold flap over

ROUND THREE: THE TEACHER-STUDENT EDITING CONFERENCE

All teachers value the opportunity to sit with their students for one-on-one instruction. Obviously, this teaching technique allows us to meet individual needs as well as possible. But realistically, the opportunities are too few due to many conditions beyond our control. So, while recognizing the logistical limitations, I advocate meeting with students, one at a time, for a five- to seven-minute mini-conference called Questioning the Writer, a title I adapted from Isabel Beck and Margaret McKeown's *Questioning the Author* (1997).

Beck and McKeown's book helped me grasp the power students possess when they are trained to question authors during reading. We can apply their concept to the revision process, in which the teacher questions the student during a rereading of a student's Round 2 draft. In this questioning process, the teacher gives the opportunity to revise—and ownership of the writing—back to the student-writer.

A Teacher's Dilemma: To Collect-and-Correct or to Confer?

It seems to me that as teachers of writing, we have two basic ways to respond to student writing. The first is the age-old collect-and-correct procedure: The teacher collects students' papers, reads them over, and marks the errors with a red pen. The good news for this approach is that students' rewrites are better due to fewer errors. The bad news is that the *same problems* usually show up on the next writing assignment. This is because collect-and-correct teachers spend their time correcting the writing instead of teaching the writer. And because of the vast amount of time it takes to read and correct papers, teachers tend to focus primarily on fixing sentence-level grammar issues. And so we miss the big picture—the developing student-writer—and often dampen his or her desire to write with passion, clarity, and finesse.

In fact, research shows that focusing exclusively on grammar in our instruction may run counter to our goals. The online University Writing Center at Cal State, Los Angeles, cites this research from George Hillocks, Jr., in *Research on Written Composition*:

> The study of traditional school grammar (i.e., the definition of parts of speech, the parsing of sentences, etc.) has no effect on raising the quality of student writing. Every other focus of instruction examined in this review is stronger. Taught in certain ways, grammar and mechanics instruction has a deleterious effect on student writing. In some studies a heavy emphasis on mechanics and usage (e.g., marking every error) resulted in significant losses in overall quality (1986).

Similarly, in its guidelines on writing, the National Council of Teachers of English (NCTE) advises

> Watch out for "the grammar trap" . . . Some knowledge of grammar is useful, but too much time spent on the study of grammar steals time from the study of writing. Time is much better spent in writing and conferring with the teacher or other students about each attempt to communicate in writing (1980).

Neither Professor Hillocks, the NCTE, nor I am suggesting that errors are okay in student writing. Grammar, punctuation, and spelling mistakes have the harmful effect of distracting the reader from the writer's important content message. It's just that we have somehow lost our balance and swung too far to the error-marking side.

In lieu of the collect-and-correct approach, I suggest that we confer with students and ask them the critical questions that help them to close the gap between the "paper in their heads" and the "paper written on the page." An editor's job is to probe, prompt, and push the writer toward the highest possible level of accuracy in his or her delivery of thoughts, ideas, experiences, opinions, reactions, or information. We can take on this role by listening to individual students read their drafts, paying close attention to the bumps in the comprehension road we experience as an early audience, and giving them focused feedback. The conference must be short—about five to seven minutes—and extremely productive. I explain my procedure and provide some troubleshooting tips below.

Conducting a Questioning-the-Writer (Q-t-W) Conference

Invite a student to work with you at your desk with his or her revised draft. Sitting next to the student, ask him or her to read the writing to you. As you follow along and listen, jot down on a piece of scratch paper questions that point to any confusions you are experiencing, any areas that cause glitches in your understanding, any parts that demand clarification.

The questions you ask will vary from student to student depending on how easily you understand the writing. When you're confused about the overall meaning, you'll pose questions that seek additional information. When you stumble over a poorly phrased point or position, you'll ask questions that seek clarification. Most of the questions you ask will target the writer's ideas and content, support and evidence, examples and details, and organization/structure. However, you'll also want to ask grammar and usage questions when phrasing and mechanics impede the communication from writer to audience. (See the Questions for a Student-Writer on page 80.)

After the student finishes reading the draft to you, and you finish jotting down your questions, gauge how much time you have and decide on a priority of questions in case you run out of time. The first question I typically ask is one that leads to a compliment for the student-writer. For example, "Where did you get the idea about _____ ?" The student tells me, and I say, "Nice. Very nice. I'll bet the author will like that part." Beginning with a positive comment sets a positive tone for the rest of the conference.

Ask each question and record the answer beneath the question. (Since you can write much faster than most students, this is a time-saver. Be sure to write quickly but neatly enough for them to be able to read it.) At the end of the conference, congratulate the student for the hard work, and present the list of questions and answers, and have them tell you their revision plan.

Here, we can ask an open-ended question like, "What will you do next?" Sometimes that means students choose to do the minimum and other times students rise to the

Questions for a Student-Writer in a Q-t-W Conference

Take a look back at the student-to-author postcard that introduced this chapter. Here are some questions I would pose to Lance about his draft in a Questioning-the-Writer conference along with my goals for each:

❊ What was it about the first scene in the story "The First Time" that you liked? Why did you like the advice to carry two $50 bills to the seller's house? Is that a strategy that you think would help a buyer get the best price?
[Goal: seek clarification; give support for opinions]

❊ Do you really think that it's possible that the author chose to make the characters nameless in order to confuse the reader? Or do you think the author had another purpose? What might it be?
[Goal: seek clarification; provide a rationale for author's choices]

❊ What is your opinion of the young buyer? Is he smart? Is he naïve? Did he get burned on the deal?
[Goal: seek expansion; analyze the character]

❊ What are your thoughts about the female character? Who is she? What was her role in the story?
[Goal: seek expansion; analyze the character]

❊ How would you rate your understanding of the story? Did you get it all or are there some parts that were confusing that you could clarify in a rewrite?
[Goal: promote metacognition; reflect on learning]

❊ What do you remember about run-on sentences and how to avoid them? The run-on in paragraph 2 distracted me.
[Goal: seek clarification; make the writing cleaner for the reader]

I ask my questions to seek understanding and to seek a path for the student to clarify the writing for the real audience—the author who will eventually receive this writing.

occasion and answer all the questions. Though we've invested some precious instructional time here, the revision has to be the student's choice because it is the student's writing. I am trying to "teach the writer, not correct the writing," so we give them the choice.

Of course, you may want to structure the send-off to include a specific commitment from the writer, for example, "What two or three things will you *commit* to change in your draft?" I understand and respect this approach, so if you prefer it, use it.

Teaching Tips for Successful Questioning-the-Writer Conferences

1. **Plan for conferences realistically.** If you have 25 or even 35 students in a class, don't panic. Accept the reality that you will not be able to confer with every student on every writing assignment. Choose five to ten students randomly or select those students whom you feel will benefit most from direct feedback and attention from you on this particular project. Record their names and the date of the conference in your grade book or lesson planner, so you'll be sure to confer with different kids next time.

For those students who don't get a conference with you, here are several options for giving them support and feedback on their drafts:

- Conduct a "remote conference" with them by collecting their drafts, reading them later, and jotting down a list of questions you need answers to. (I use sticky-notes instead of scratch paper here, so that the questions can be affixed on the draft right where the confusion occurred.) Students answer my questions and then decide what to do about it.

- Instruct students to find an "adult editor surrogate" to take your place. This is any adult who is kind enough to spend ten to 15 minutes with the student conferring about the paper. Of course, any adult, be it a parent, guardian, older sibling, another teacher, coach, or clergyperson, willing to take this on will need some help pulling off a Questioning-the-Writer response; otherwise they will likely do the sort of traditional editing job they remember their teachers doing for them. To avoid the error-marking approach, provide students

You can find the letter I use to guide the adults students chose as their surrogate editors at http://www.larrylewin.com/books. As you draft your letter, you may also want to use this quote from the NCTE's guidelines for parents on "How to Help Your Child Become a Better Writer":

"Be primarily interested in the content, not the mechanics of expression. It's easy for many adults to spot misspellings, faulty word usage, and shaky punctuation. Perfection in these areas escapes most adults, so don't demand it of children. Sometimes teachers—for the same reason—will mark only a few mechanical errors, leaving others for another time. What matters most in writing is words, sentences, and ideas. Perfection in mechanics develops slowly. Be patient." (1980).

with a cover letter to accompany the draft. The letter should walk the surrogate through a procedure for questioning the writer. You may want to assure this wonderful surrogate editor that you will be taking one last look at the papers to deal with the mechanics back in class (Round 4, below).

2. **Lay down the law on student behavior.** The best way for this teaching technique to fail is for the other students in the class to be off-task and interruptive. When you conduct a conference, you'll need 100 percent focused attention on the student and the writing, so that you can quickly recognize the confusing parts and jot them on the scratch paper. If two kids are messing around across the room, your attention focuses on them rather than the conference. No good. Likewise, having three or four kids milling around your desk asking, "Is it my turn yet?" is too distracting. Establish a set of class rules for conference time, and train students to follow them from the start. See my Rules for Writing Conference Time on page 83 for an example.

3. **Try it and refine it.** Learning how to confer with student-writers in this question-asking mode isn't easy. It takes time to learn to do it quickly and effectively. Consider piloting it with a few of your more cooperative students who might catch on to the routine easily and gratefully. Also, you may want to set up a role play in which you and a selected student go through a conference again, modeling it for the class. Finally, since it is so different from the alternative method, give yourself enough tries at it to become comfortable. Don't give it up prematurely.

Round 4: A Call for the Editor in Chief

Yes, we can institute a fourth Round of Repair when it's needed. While I believe the collect-and-correct approach does not help students in the first three rounds, I also believe we must address student writing errors before we send off or otherwise present their responses to critical readers; to ignore them would be unfair to students.

Here's my solution: Round 4 is called "The Editor in Chief," and it's the time when the teacher collects the reworked drafts from rounds 1, 2, and 3, bites the bullet, and pulls out the red (or green) pen to mark any remaining problems.

Clearly this is "correcting the writing" and not "teaching the writer." But wait: It *is* teaching the writer—it demonstrates that quality writing gets a final polishing from an editor who knows the rules of the road. Every article and book I have ever published received the final scrutiny of a highly skilled text editor who attacked the remaining pesky errors and "bugs" in my writing, wielding a red pen like a can of Raid. And I was thankful.

Tell students, "The last thing I want to see happen here is for you to be embarrassed in front of the author because you don't know some apostrophe rule, or you misspelled a word." What we don't tell them is that the real last thing we want to happen is for *us* to be embarrassed that our students haven't mastered the writing conventions. It looks bad, very bad.

Rules for Writing Conference Time

We need full cooperation from a class in order to conduct writing conferences. So, classroom rules apply. Students must be trained on how to behave during conference time. Here are some ground rules you can adapt for your own students:

When I'm conferring with a writer, please do the following:

1. Work quietly without talking at your desk. I need your total, complete, 100 percent cooperation on this.

2. Write any questions you have about the assignment on one of the blue question slips I have set out for you. Put it in the basket for me, and I'll get to you after the current conference is over. Meanwhile, work on another part of the assignment quietly; be productive.

3. If you finish your "first dare" while I'm in a conference, do one (or more) of these:
   - begin a Sentence Opening Sheet (S.O.S.)
   - begin an illustration to accompany your paper
   - study your spelling list
   - read your book

4. Sign your name on the board if you want a conference with me and you have completed your S.O.S. I will get to you as soon as I can . . . maybe today or maybe not. Please be patient; I am working as hard as I can.

5. If you want to have a peer partner editor, let me know before a conference begins so that I can find a quiet place for you two.

6. If today is looking like a bad day for you and you doubt that you will be able to follow all these directions, please just say so before we begin so that I can find another location for you to work this period and we can avoid negative consequences.

The key is clear, explicit expectations, accompanied by training students for independent work, and seriously following up with consequences for noncompliers.

Adapted from *Paving the Way in Reading and Writing: Strategies and Activities to Support Struggling Students in Grades 6–12*
© Larry Lewin. Jossey-Bass, 2003.

And it is embarrassing. Readers have no tolerance for mistakes. If this paragraph you're reading has a typo or a grammar error, then you no doubt will see it and say "tsk, tsk," and probably lose some confidence in me. It's true, isn't it? Mechanical errors overpower the content. It doesn't seem fair, but it must be human nature because all readers notice them.

So, I tell students this sad truth, and I tell them we will not allow a few mistakes to devalue the power of the words we've worked so hard to set down on paper. We will prevent this by being considerate of our audience. We will keep the audience's eye on our message—where it belongs.

I read all papers for publication carefully and mark the remaining errors. They go back to the students who take out a fresh sheet of paper and rewrite carefully because this is the version that the author will be reading. This is the final, finished, polished paper. It's show time.

BACK TO ROUND 0

The good news is not every writing assignment we make must go through the Rounds of Repair. On the contrary, many writing assignments may only go through Round 1, or Rounds 1 and 2. And some assignments will not receive any repair work and remain a rough draft.

This is because not every assignment will be sent out of the classroom to a real audience. I've advocated helping students produce meaningful writing to send to real audiences, but mailing the responses doesn't happen *all the time*. It cannot happen all the time because we sometimes run out of time and have to move on to another topic, or the author of the assigned reading is deceased, or we lacked time and energy to search for the author's address.

This is okay, but if you want to capitalize on the powerful effect "talking back" to authors has on students, plan to send student-to-author feedback writing at some point. And when students' work will be published and sent to the intended audience, I strongly recommend four Rounds of Repair.

———————————— ❖ ————————————

A paper is never finished. There is always another version of it to write.

I hate to tell students this, but it's true. No piece of writing is ever finally finished. Rather, there always comes a time to stop the writing, and the rewriting and rewriting. The time is known as a deadline, and all writers recognize this necessity. I even show students an article I had published in a teacher journal or a book I wrote, and I ask, "Is this writing done?" They of course say, "Yes, it's published. It's out there."

"True," I say, "but there are a few things in it that I don't feel too good about. And if I could, I would happily take it back and improve it. But the deadline came, and I had to stop working on it and let it go. It was good, maybe even very good but certainly not perfect. I wish is was perfect, but it's not."

In school, it's the same thing. We will give our writing our best shot, but in time we will have to release it to the audience. But before we set it free, we will give it a chance, several chances, to be the best it can be.

In this chapter we considered a revision and editing approach called Three Rounds of Repair, and I provided a set of teaching tips for self-editing, peer editing, and teacher-student conferring. I suggested adding a fourth round before the papers leave the classroom, and I noted that, depending on the assignment's audience and purpose, sometimes no repairing is necessary. And that's okay. The goal is to convince our students that editing, rewriting, revision, proofreading, whatever we call it, has a purpose, and that purpose is not punishment. The purpose is to be a considerate writer who wants to make the communication with the audience the best it can be.

And after we rework the drafts and make them the best they can be, we evaluate the writing and mail them to the author-audience. How we accomplish this is addressed in the next two chapters.

CHAPTER 4

ASSESSING STUDENTS' FEEDBACK WRITING

We're out for students' successes, not just to document their deficiencies.

—Rick Wormeli

At the end of the revision process, students are eager to show off their polished postcards, memos, or letters. Now is a good time to evaluate them. I recommend three grading options: giving credit for completion, awarding percentage points, and scoring papers with a special rubric, called a ChecBric.

Option 1: Congratulations for Completion

Because the reading-writing approach I am advocating—teaching critical reading through student-to-author writing—is new to most of us, and especially new to students, we may opt to give credit to students who complete the assignment, rather than conduct a formal evaluation of their work. This could be as simple as checking off a completion mark in your grade book, or marking off a number of points earned, say 50 or 100 (whatever you decide the assignment is worth).

The obvious benefits to this method are its rapidity and simplicity: Students know that if they complete their student-to-author writing assignment, they automatically earn a certain number of points. Not only is this easy on the teacher's time, it simply says, "We tried something new. You did it. I congratulate you."

The obvious deficiency to this method is it ignores the degree of proficiency students have achieved. All their work is equally valued. Because there will be a wide range in the quality of student-written responses, let's look at Option 2.

Option 2: Using an Assessment List

An assessment list, sometimes known as a criterion-referenced performance list, does two things for students: It lists the requirements (criteria) of an assignment, and it allots point values to each criterion.

For example, if you were to create an assessment list for a student-to-author P-Q-P memo, you might begin with these:

1. praise for the author
2. questions for the author
3. polishing suggestions for the author

These three criteria are the requirements you've established for a successful P-Q-P memo. Likely, you've already introduced and modeled these qualities for students early in the assignment.

Beside each criterion on the assessment list, you would post the maximum point value to be earned for each one. You may decide that the praise section of the memo is worth 25 points, the questions to the author are worth 25 points, and the suggested improvements for polishing are worth 25 points, making this writing assignment worth 75 points max as shown below.

Assessment List for a P-Q-P		
Requirements	**Point Value**	**Points Earned**
1. praise for the author	25 points	_____
2. questions for the author	25 points	_____
3. polishing suggestions for the author	25 points	_____
Total 75 points		_____

Alternatively, you may determine that the criteria are not equally valued and therefore allot a different point value for each. For instance, if you think the polishing requirement is the most demanding or challenging aspect of the P-Q-P assignment, then you may want to allocate 30 or 35 points. Or if you typically score student writing assignments on a 25-point scale, then the three criteria might be: 5 points for praise, 8 points for questions, and 12 points for polishes.

Two benefits of this evaluation technique are that it reinforces students' understanding of the specific expectations of the assignment and they recognize which element(s) you value most. This understanding can guide their work and help them create a better piece of writing.

A third benefit of using assessment lists is for the teacher: You can easily convert the points earned for the criteria into a percentage for a letter grade. For example, if the total number of points valued for an assignment is 75, and the student's total number of points is 62, the percent earned is computed by dividing 62 by 75 to get 82 percent, which on most grading scales converts into a B-. Of course, you can save yourself some math time by designing your assessment list to total 10 points or 100 points. But don't forget, if you weighted the criteria differently, then you have some math to do.

The downside to using an assessment list is determining a point value for the criteria in each student's work. For example, would you judge Carissa's questions to the author on page 7 as worth 6, 7, or 8 out of 8 points maximum? This could be a bit subjective, right? And what would you tell her if she asked you why she earned a 7 instead of an 8? Even though you would be scoring a class set of P-Q-Ps and you'd have some examples to show her in support of your judgment, this method can be tough to defend.

Further, the number of criteria is just as open to personal choice as the allotment of point values. In response to my decision to use three criteria in the P-Q-P memo assignment above, you may have thought, "Well, what about providing support for an opinion with examples from the reading, using the proper tone of voice, structuring the writing with paragraphs, neat handwriting, or correct spelling?" Certainly, you'll want to include those elements that you know will provide the best picture of a successful student response. Keep in mind, though, that the more criteria you include, the more responsibilities students have to handle, and the more scoring you'll need to do. While I do not prescribe a magic number of criteria and the perfect point values, I can tell you that three work best for me and the students I teach.

Option 3: ChecBrics

Introduced in Chapter 1 and reviewed in Chapter 2, a ChecBric is a hybrid scoring device that merges a checklist with a rubric: Chec + Bric = ChecBric. This third assessment option is the one I recommend most because it overcomes the problems associated with the first two methods: It measures students' proficiency in response writing and awards points more objectively than an assessment list.

I create a ChecBric for students by first deciding the criteria for a successful student-to-author writing assignment. First I create the student's side: the checklist. On the left column of a sheet of paper, I list the chosen criteria, calling them "targets." Beneath each target I include a short checklist that fully describes the requirements for meeting that criterion/target in language students can understand. Students like checklists because they are easy to use: Read the requirements and check them off as you complete them.

Then I create the scoring side, a rubric, in the right column for my use. If you use rubrics to assess student work, you know the benefits: detailed expectations for work quality, clear point values assigned to different levels of work quality, and objective scoring.

For example, when we look at sixth grader Carissa's memo to me and assess her ability to ask questions, we can apply the Target/Trait 2 to this part of her response:

> I didn't really understand why you put what Sidd's tail looks like (para. 14, lines 6–7). And why did you worry what your face looked like (para. 14, line 7) when you can't see it when the black light is not on? How do cats wear glasses?

Target 2: I Question the Author	Trait 2: Seeks Clarifications
❑ My memo asks for more information. ❑ My memo asks for clarification. ❑ My memo asks about why the author made certain choices.	4 = Advanced: deep, insightful, or profound questions 3 = Proficient: adequate, interesting, or useful questions 2 = Basic: obvious, generic, or common-place questions 1 = Below Basic: limited, naïve, or irrelevant questions

Carissa's questions in her second paragraph are specific to the story, not generic or commonplace like "What made you want to write?" or "Where do you get ideas for your stories?" She asks for clarification ("I don't really understand why . . . "). She is clearly over the hump up at a 3—proficient. Her other questions delve into the author's choices, "Why did you worry . . . ?" And she goes further in her analysis by providing citations to examples in the story. If we decide from our observations of her previous performance feel that these are "deep, insightful, or profound," we might raise her score to a 4—advanced. Carissa earns a 3 or a 4 (with any rubric a 1-point difference of opinion is acceptable).

Textbook Chapter Rewrite ChecBric

Student Checklist

Target 1: The information I summarized in my chapter rewrite is **accurate, thorough, and easy to understand.**

- ❏ 1. I have correctly identified the **key points** of the chapter.
- ❏ 2. I have correctly defined the **key terms**.
- ❏ 3. I have correctly shown the **key equations**.
- ❏ 4. I have **prioritized** the information without sacrificing essential points.
- ❏ 5. I have made the information easy to **understand** for myself and my audience.

Target 2: My version of this chapter is **better than the original.**

- ❏ 1. I have improved the teaching of the **key points** of the chapter.
- ❏ 2. I have improved the **examples.**
- ❏ 3. I have improved the **layout.** [See Hint 1]
- ❏ 4. I have improved the **language.** [See Hint 2]

Target 3: I have been **courteous to my readers** when writing my chapter.

- ❏ 1. I have checked my **spelling.**
- ❏ 2. I have been careful with **punctuation and capitalization.**
- ❏ 3. I have **written or printed neatly.**
- ❏ 4. I have indented for **new paragraphs.**

Teacher Rubric

Trait 1: Content Understanding

4 = Advanced: compelling, thorough understanding of the chapter's information

3 = Proficient: adequate summary of the chapter's information

2 = Basic: overly broad or simplistic understanding of the chapter's information

1 = Below Basic: minimal, disorganized description, or unclear understanding of the chapter's information

Trait 2: Improvement

4 = Advanced: outstanding portrayal of the chapter; superior to the original

3 = Proficient: adequate portrayal of the chapter; preferable to the original

2 = Basic: inadequate portrayal of the chapter; little or no improvement on the original

1 = Below Basic: minimal or weak portrayal of the chapter; inferior to the original

Trait 3: Editing

4 = Advanced: outstanding control of the writing conventions; the writing enhances the rewritten chapter for the audience

3 = Proficient: adequate control of the writing conventions; errors are minor and do not distract the audience from the rewritten chapter

2 = Basic: inadequate control of the writing conventions; errors are present and begin to interrupt the audience's understanding of the rewritten chapter

1 = Below Basic: lack of control of the writing conventions; errors are frequent or significant to cause a breakdown in the audience's understanding of the rewritten chapter

Name _____ Date _____

Textbook Chapter Rewrite ChecBric
(continued)

Student Checklist

Hint 1: The **Layout** of my booklet presents my information in a **user-friendly** manner.

❑ 1. I have laid out/designed the rewrite in an attractive way.

❑ 2. I have included helpful **illustrations**, either copied or drawn by hand.

❑ 3. I have either written in cursive, printed, or typed the words **neatly**.

❑ 4. I have added **special print** to enhance my booklet, such as color or boldface.

Hint 2: The **language** I have used in my chapter is **clear, interesting, and student-friendly** for my audience.

❑ 1. I have rewritten the book's words into more **student-friendly language**.

❑ 2. I have **paraphrased** the book's language in my own words.

❑ 3. Where I have **copied** the book's exact words, I have cited them properly.

❑ 4. Where appropriate, I have added some **humor** to help deliver the information.

Student reflections on the assignment:

_____

_____

_____

_____

_____

_____

_____

Teacher Rubric

Presentation

4 = Advanced: very pleasing layout design with engaging visuals

3 = Proficient: layout design and visuals work well to support the chapter rewrite's information

2 = Basic: layout design and visuals while present, do not succeed in supporting the chapter rewrite's information

1 = Below Basic: layout design or visuals are messy, confusing, unappealing; they interfere with the chapter rewrite's information

Use of Language

4 = Advanced: strong, precise, engaging words make chapter rewrite clear; excellent paraphrasing; correct citations; may show some humor

3 = Proficient: good, appropriate words make chapter rewrite clear; evidence of paraphrasing; some citations; may show some humor

2 = Basic: inadequate word choice, paraphrasing, and citations; use of language interferes with chapter rewrite

1 = Below Basic: words chosen cause confusion; lots of copied language from the text without proper citations

Teacher comments to student:

_____

_____

_____

_____

_____

_____

_____

_____

_____

_____

_____

_____

The ChecBric format is also a great way to scaffold students' evaluations of their own writing. How many times have we assembled a labor-intensive rubric and presented it to a class only to see their eyes glaze over? The problem with using rubrics alone is that they typically are very detailed and written in teacher language, which is tough for most students to understand. However, placing a checklist alongside the rubric affords an opportunity for students to understand our grading plan and to attempt their own evaluation. Once they are accustomed to the tool, you may even want to push students to score their work before you collect it, as in the example below.

A ChecBric in Action

Take a look at a ChecBric I cocreated with Kevin Callahan for his pre-algebra students' rewrite of their math textbook. I told the seventh and eighth graders in Kevin's class: "The checklist is for you. Look at it in the left column and find out how many 'targets' you are expected to hit in this assignment." A quick glance at the checklist (page 90) showed students that the assignment had three targeted requirements, along with two additional hints (page 91).

Next I asked them, "Who can explain what Target 1, 'The information I summarized in the chapter is accurate, thorough, and easy to understand,' means." This was a bit more challenging to the students, so we discussed the meaning of *accurate* as being correct, not wrong. For *thorough* one kid offered a useful synonym, *complete*, while another used an antonym, *not half-baked*. (In fact, sometimes students come up with more easily understandable terminology. Each time you use it, you'll want to revise a ChecBric's language to better meet student needs.)

Then I told them, "Notice that there is a handy-dandy checklist beneath Target 1 for you to use to make sure you hit the target." After going over the remaining two targets and checklist items, I gave them a strategy for using the checklist: "Be smart and use the checklist for each target three times: First, before you begin writing, use the checklist items to review this assignment's requirements. Then, while you are writing, check off the requirements as you complete them, and finally, after you finish writing, go back and double-check the items to make sure you hit the targets."

Some students equate hard work with a high score on the rubric. I recommend conferring with a student whose projected point scores are higher than the earned score you give. Help him or her understand that effort doesn't automatically translate into good performance; say to the student, "It's great that you were shooting for the highest score. To earn those scores, here are some things you needed to do. Let's look at them first on the ChecBric. Then let's see if they are in your writing." Let the student find specific areas of accomplishment and help them compare what they've achieved so far to what you expect for the high score they're aiming for.

After some discussion and modeling, I pointed out the rubric with the 6-point scoring scale and explained to students that the rubric is for the teachers to score how well they, the writers, hit the targets. In Oregon where these students attend school, the state assessments use a 6-point scoring scale, so they are familiar with the scoring system and know that a 6 indicates an exceptional job, a 5 is very good, a 4 shows proficiency, and so on.

Finally, I told them, "The rubric side of the ChecBric is for Mr. Callahan and me. It's a way for us to score your textbook rewrites, but if you want to peek over the middle dividing line and look at the rubric, that's fine. And I've actually seen some students circle the score they think they have earned for each trait, which is what teachers call the *targets*."

The first time they use the ChecBric, I gently nudge students toward self-evaluation as in the example above, with the goal of introducing self-evaluation as an option. Then, later when I hand out the ChecBric for another assignment, I might say to them, "Who remembers what a ChecBric is used for? Which side is your side? Which side is my side? . . . Well, this time both sides are your side, so use the Checklist to check off the requirements as you complete them, and then use the Rubric side to circle the score you predict you'll be earning for each target/trait." Now they are ready to move into self-assessment.

> If you are interested in learning more about ChecBrics, look for Great Performances (ASCD, 1998), a guide on classroom-based assessment I coauthored with my colleague Bette Shoemaker. You can also find more examples of ChecBrics on my Web site www.larrylewin.com/books. Feel free to copy any that look promising, paste them into your word processor, and then adapt them to meet your needs.

ChecBric Development: Time Well Spent

A ChecBric is well worth the time it takes to create and use. Students appreciate the student-friendly language of the checklist and the reminder of the requirements for the assignment—they produce better work in the end. The rubric column connects a classroom-based assessment to the state's rubric point score and it provides a more objective evaluation from the teacher. It also invites students to assess their own work against high standards.

And it's a simple tool to revise for new assignments: Once you've created a ChecBric with your word processor and saved it, not only can you easily edit it for improvement, you can copy and paste selected lines into a new ChecBric for another assignment. I also recommend using language from either your district or state's official scoring rubrics when creating the second column. If the rubric is available on your district or State Department of Education's Web site, simply copy and paste it in.

Reality Check:
Last Thoughts on Assessment ✛✛✛✛✛✛✛✛✛✛✛✛

When assessing student response writing, bear in mind that you may encounter some disappointments. Here are three that I've experienced, along with strategies to deal with them fairly:

First, a student-to-author critique is sometimes more about the student than about the reading-writing assignment. Despite our best efforts at motivating reading and writing with this "talk-back" approach, some students may still harbor negativity to writing back to the author. Don't be shocked if a kid is feeling grouchy or grumpy, and it comes through in the writing. You may rightfully feel disappointed when reading such a response, but go ahead and assess it. Don't let your disappointment taint your scoring. Stick to the criteria, and score the writing based on what you set up as the required traits.

Also, don't let your feelings get hurt if some students identify more areas in need of polish than praises for the author. Even though we may love a particular short story, novel, article, textbook chapter, or Web site, it is unrealistic to expect every student in our classes to feel the same. Each reader has the right to react as she or he feels. So, be cool when confronted by a student's analysis of more negative and less positive. Just score the required "praise" comments low because they are weak. The "polish" comments will earn a higher score because they are stronger. That's what an *analytical trait* scoring is about: Give each student specific feedback on the various aspects (traits) of the assignment.

Finally, you may occasionally receive an idiosyncratic response to an author in which the student uses the writing assignment to explore issues that have little to do with the author's writing. For example, seventh grader Acacia used her P-Q-P letter to tell author Gary Soto about her favorite music. In the suggestions-for-polishing paragraph, she urges him to write stories about "modern-day music, like my favorite bands Green Day, My Chemical Romance, The Used. . . ." Her scores on the "praise" and "questions" targets were necessarily low, because she wrote very little in these paragraphs, but her score for "polishing" was better because she did offer suggestions for improvements, as weird as they were. It probably would be a bit odd for the author to read a memo like this. Tough call: Send it and let the kid be heard or don't send it due to a lack of focus. I opted to send it.

Before the memos, postcards, or letters get sent out of the classroom, we can, and should, assess them to offer students our feedback on what worked and didn't work in their writing. As with any writing assignment in school, students can benefit from the evaluation of their teacher— and also from the expectations laid out by that assessment.

Teachers, as well, benefit from assessment because it serves to inform us about where each student is currently, what aspects of the assignment were successful, what aspects still need work. Good assessment informs our instruction. With evaluations of the polished work completed, student responses are ready to send to the author. Chapter 5 provides help in getting the writing from students' desks to the author's mailbox.

CHAPTER 5

COMPLETING THE READER-WRITER CIRCLE

I like your story because it's very funny. It's hilarious, especially when the main character gets the orange goo all over his face. I think you should have another pet story about a frog that has to go to the vet to get his warts removed.
—Prescott, grade 6

Prescott, I am pleased that you found the story hilarious. I have never received a memo from a student reader who used that word. I appreciate it very much. I don't think I can write a story about a frog unless I have some help. Do you want to start writing it?
—the author's response

When sixth grader Jesus was assigned a feedback-to-the-author memo, one thing he chose to do was to ask the author a few questions about the story. He wrote:

> I want to ask what gave you the inspiration to write this story? And I was curious about the other character's name, I mean the owner of the cat. And did you come up with all the ideas, or did someone help you? . . .

It is exciting to me when young readers are emboldened to make inquiries to authors. I especially am excited by Jesus's questions because I am the author of the story his teacher Christine Gonzalez assigned (see Chapter 1). Jesus's questions about my process and choices helps to break down the wall between reader and writer. His classmate Liliana wrote me a memo and asked, "Do you have any cats or any other pets? If you do, do you take them to the vet? Do they like the vet?" I can tell from her questions where she's headed: She wants to know how realistic my short story "Sidd's Excellent Adventure" is.

I'm thrilled when students contact me with memos, postcards, and letters because I enjoy hearing them "talk back" to authors. And you know that I will not let the circle be broken—I always write back. (See my response on page 98.) And since I have not yet published my fiction writing, I am not overwhelmed by fan mail at present. I get some great responses from students whose teachers use my stories after reading them in one of my workshops, and responding is manageable for me. However, not all authors write back to students.

In this chapter we consider the logistical issues of publishing student-to-author writing: contacting authors and sending student writing to them, and increasing the chances of receiving a reply from the author.

Contacting Authors to Send Student Responses

Let me be very direct about this: I believe that any published author who receives mail from student readers has the obligation to reply. Yes, an *obligation*.

Writers write for their audience. Without the audience, authors would not be published—no published works, no paycheck. So, when a member of the audience takes the time to write to the author, that author should find the time to write back—keeping the communication circle from breaking.

You'll notice in my letter to Christina's sixth graders that I took the time to write a detailed, specific response, not a generic "thanks for writing; be sure to read lots of good books; have a nice day" form letter.

You'll also notice that I wrote my letter to the whole class, not individual, customized letters to each student. I'm a good guy to take the time to write back, but I don't have unlimited time to write 29 letters. Fair enough, right? Some authors are so popular that they get inundated with mail. To expect famous authors to write a specific, precise letter back to the class is unrealistic.

The good news is that I've found many real authors who agree with my position. Even with their busy schedules they take the time to write back to kids. This is the right thing to do. But let's tackle first things first: Where should we send students' writing to reach the author?

An Author Responds to a Class

In this letter to Ms. Gonzalez's class, I answer several common questions students asked about my story "Sidd's Excellent Adventure" in their response memos. I also address their interest in the fact- and fiction-based parts of the narrative and ask them for feedback on a revised version of the story, based on their questions and comments.

Dear Ms. Gonzalez and Students,

Thank you very much for reading my story "Sidd's Excellent Adventure" and writing me your memos.

Many of you asked where I got the story idea.

It is a true story that happened to me. Well, I should say that it starts as a true story that really happened, but then, as you know, it turns into a fantasy. The fantasy begins at the point in the vet's examination room where the narrator puts the orange goo onto the cat's tail and his face. I am proud to say that I did not really do either of those things. Now, I admit to THINKING about smearing it onto Sidd and myself, but because I am a mature, responsible adult of over 50 years, I decided not to do it.

The orange goo and black light are true; the vet really did that to Sidd, and it was very cool to see it. The orange smoochie to Inga (my wife's real name is Linda, but I changed it in the story) did not happen either, although it would have been funny to try.

Sidd is a real cat we adopted years ago. He showed up on our doorstep meowing for food and love, but since we already had Dolores (my cat who lived to be 19 years old), I said no to Linda. But of course she didn't listen, and after four days, she invited Sidd into our house.

About a week later we learned that Sidd was owned by a man from Montana who was visiting his brother—a neighbor of ours from up the street. Since the brother had two big dogs, Sidd decided to check out other places. He picked us because, I believe, cats can tell who their friends are. The man from Montana was traveling and looking to move somewhere new, so he decided to let Sidd stay with us. He told us that Sidd was short for Siddhartha, and that he was an amazing cat. He first had lived in an apartment, and his first owner didn't appreciate his claws on the furniture, so she had the vet remove them. Later, Sidd was given to him, but he lived out in the wild woods, and Sidd had no front claws for defense. Somehow he managed to survive. Later, after he moved in with us, I saw him climb a tree to escape a raccoon—without front claws! Pretty good.

Later we were shocked when we learned that Sidd was not a He, but a She. She was a very beautiful, sweet, and wonderful housemate for years. We had to put her to sleep after she became blind and deaf in her old age.

I write stories about things I have seen or done, but I usually change them by adding new things to try to make them more interesting to readers. In fact, after reading your memos, I decided to rewrite this story to change the narrator from me into a 12-year-old boy assisting his mother. It is renamed "Sidd, the Super Cat." Read it, and let me know which version you prefer.

Best wishes,

Larry Lewin

Finding the Author's Address on the Internet

I use the Web to locate authors. It is generally much faster than applying the old-fashioned technique of using the publisher's postal address. That method is slow because the publisher serves as a middleperson. (Of course, if this is the only route you can find, I suggest writing very early in the assignment to give yourself three weeks for the package of student letters to make its way to the author. Address the letter to the author, care of the publisher, whose address you can find on the back of the book's title page.)

But I usually succeed in finding contact information for authors on the Internet. One way I look is to go to a search engine, such as Google (www.google.com) and type in the author's name and "home page" or "official site." I discovered Jean Craighead George's site (www.jeancraigheadgeorge.com) in this way. While George's site contains no mailing address, toward the bottom of her home page is her e-mail address and a note to readers who wish to contact her (at right).

Email: jeangeorgemail@aol.com

I am not a very reliable e-mail correspondent.
I try to answer everyone, but my schedule is heavy and I'm off and going places.
But know that I love to hear from you even if I can't answer.
Thank you all for your thoughts!
P.S.-If you do send me e-mail, please make sure that your return e-mail address is correct so that I can respond to you. Thank you!

Jean

I am impressed that George offers her reading public access to her e-mail. Even though she admits she is "not a very reliable e-mail correspondent," this is a connection that can help us get our students' writing to her. We could send an e-mail informing her that our students have read her book, analyzed it, and have written letters (or postcards or memos) to her expressing their critical reviews. We could also ask her where to send these important responses. E-mail can really speed up the communication process. When the author reads the teacher's inquiry e-mail and replies fairly promptly, we can get the ball rolling for mailing out the kids' work.

Receiving a letter from an author in response to students' writing is well worth the effort of some smart online searching, as Julie Janecka at Lynn Middle School in Las Cruces, New Mexico, discovered. Her students read *The Circuit* by Francisco Jiménez, a book about the author's early life with his family on the migrant agricultural circuit. Julie's search turned up Jiménez's Web site, which is hosted by Santa Clara University where he works. They sent their letters, and he wrote back.

> Another type of contact information you might find on an author's Web site is an address for book orders. I've actually had success mailing a letter to Gary Soto by sending it to the postal contact address.

> Dear Ms. Janecka and Students:
>
> You cannot imagine how pleased I was to receive your wonderful letters.
> I thoroughly enjoyed reading and sharing them with my family.
>
> Thank you, Ms. Janecka, for introducing "The Circuit" to your students.
> And thank you, students, for your positive reactions to my story. . . .

This published author and university professor concludes with "I am grateful to all of you." The students are rewarded by this author's sincere thanks.

We can't expect every student to write to every author whose work they read. That is not necessary. Communicating with authors needn't occur constantly, but every once in a while it helps developing readers read better by providing them with the reminder that printed words on a page are put there for them by an author who wants to tell them something important.

Web Sites Worth Investigating

Always try the author's Web site first, but if that doesn't provide you with either an e-mail or postal address, you can look elsewhere on the Web. There are a number of teacher resource sites that provide author contact information, such as these:

- **Index to Internet Sites: Children's and Young Adults' Authors & Illustrators** by Inez Ramsey at the Internet School Library Media Center, James Madison University at http://falcon.jmu.edu/~ramseyil/biochildhome.htm

  Dr. Ramsey has links to hundreds of authors. Click on the letter of the author's last name to be routed to a set of Web sites about the author.

- **Mona Kerby's Children's Corner** sponsored by the Carroll County Public Library in Westminster, Maryland, at http://www.carr.org/authco

  You'll find a list of 50 links to authors, including Jane Yolen.

- **The Children's Literature Web Guide** at the University of Calgary at http://www.acs.ucalgary.ca/%7Edkbrown/authors.html

  Brown offers a long list of authors' Web sites. He has catalogued them alphabetically by last names into A–J, K–P, and Q–Z.

- **Scholastic's Book Central** at http://www.scholastic.com/titles/authors

  This site has a list of Scholastic authors and illustrators along with links to their Web sites.

- **Author Link** on the Internet Public Library's Kidspace site at http://www.ipl.org/div/kidspace/askauthor/AuthorLinks.html

  This site has a list of 22 famous writers' Web sites.

Be persistent, and be clever on the Web. Keep trying, and I predict you'll be able to find the author's address. This is also true for textbook authors.

LOCATING TEXTBOOK AUTHORS

Usually, this is a simple task. In the front of any textbook, the publisher includes a page about the team of authors who wrote the book. Often each contributing author has a photo and a short bio. Note the college, university, or school district where they work, and then go the Web to conduct a search to locate the author.

University Web sites frequently offer a link directly to faculty-member information or to the academic department home pages, which have links to information about each faculty member in the department. Usually, either of these routes will get you to a page about the professor, and typically an e-mail address is provided. You might also use the search box at the top of the university home page. If this turns up nothing, return to the Web and use a search engine. Type into the search field any of these combinations:

- the name of the university with which the author is affiliated and the author's name
- the title of the textbook and the author's name
- the name of the publisher and the author's name

Use the same procedure for authors of language arts, science, social studies, art, or any other content-area textbook. Use the Internet to find the author's address or e-mail. Then make the contact.

Getting Authors to Reply to Students

Now we will consider two ways to increase the chances of an author actually writing back to our students: contacting the author in advance and assigning less famous local or in-state authors. I will also address dealing with deceased authors and offer some suggestions for handling students' disappointment if the author does not write back.

CONTACTING THE AUTHOR IN ADVANCE OF THE MAILING

Once you locate the author's contact information, *pave the way* for successful student-author communication by contacting the author first to politely give him or her a heads-up that the reviews are coming. The chances of an author responding to students increases when you do. We might call this "downfield blocking" for our students. This strategy works particularly well for textbook authors, who rarely hear from their young readers.

Once you've located the author's e-mail address (or mailing address if it's the only one available), write a note to the author explaining the following:

- you have selected his or her work for your class to read
- you want students to interact with the writing in a way that motivates them to enjoy and learn from it
- you are teaching critical-evaluation skills
- you have assigned students to write a feedback memo (or postcard or letter) to the author to achieve these goals

Ask the author if he or she would be willing to read the students' responses. In your note, you may also want to recognize the author's busy schedule, tell him or her you don't expect a personal reply to individual students, and ask what you can do to facilitate this exercise.

Give an approximate arrival date for the materials and request the proper mailing address and close with a note of thanks. Thank the author profusely for assisting in teaching your students to read and write better, which should appeal to their interest in promoting literacy. For an example of a letter written in advance to a textbook author, see page 103.

USING LOCAL OR REGIONAL AUTHORS

Another way to increase the likelihood of an author writing back is to have students read and respond to the work of writers who live close by and may be less inundated with fan mail than nationally recognized authors.

There are many, many talented young-adult authors who have not hit the big time. If you don't know any in your area, I suggest asking the media specialist in your building or the children's librarian at your public library.

Of course, we are not only looking for authors who are likely to respond to our students. We are also looking for quality writing that will engage our students. It is not enough that an author would have the time and interest in writing back about her work; the work itself must be worthy of our instruction.

Lastly, when assigning a local or regional author, not only do your chances for a written reply increase, so do your chances of having the author visit your class for an in-person dialogue.

Preparing Nonfiction Authors for Student Responses

When students contact nonfiction authors, the authors may be surprised. Unlike literature authors, who are accustomed to receiving mail from students, the authors of textbooks, magazine and newspaper articles, brochures, and Web resources usually do not hear from young readers. Yours may even be the first class to contact a nonfiction author, which is all the more reason for you to contact the author(s) in advance to share what your students are doing. You want the author to understand the purpose of this venture, and you want to not catch him or her off-guard with an envelope full of student feedback writing, which critiques the author's writing and demands a response.

Here is an e-mail Kevin Callahan, a pre-algebra teacher at Madison Middle School in Eugene, Oregon, sent to the lead author of the math textbook he and his students used:

Dear Professor L_____,

I teach pre-algebra at Madison Middle School in Eugene, Oregon. I use your textbook *Middle School Math, Course 3* with success, and I wanted to share an idea with you.

My seventh and eighth graders in the course were assigned Chapter 11: Linear Equations and Graphs in June. I divided them into teams of three students with the task of rewriting a section of the chapter as a study guide.

The purpose of this assignment is to move them up to the higher levels of thinking in Bloom's Taxonomy. In order to rewrite the text, the students must understand the content information very well. They had to critique your presentation, they had to determine which aspects they benefited from, and they had to attempt to improve upon it. [I believe my students' study guides add meaning to] the text for themselves, their classmates, my future pre-algebra students, and maybe even a wider audience.

This is a very demanding exercise, and one that my students initially were uncomfortable with. But I assured them that I would provide them with a solid structure and lots of help. . . .

I would like to mail you a few samples from my students for your feedback. Please let me know if you are interested, and if so, provide me with your mailing address.

Thanks very much,

Kevin Callahan

The Issue of Deceased Authors

Do you know the book *The Pigman* by Paul Zindel? A classic coming-of-age account of two teenagers, this novel has been on high school literature lists for decades. Students read it and they love it. It's a perfect book for talking back to the author. The problem is, Mr. Zindel passed away in 2003.

I found this out the hard way. I received an e-mail from Mary Mendivil, a teacher who attended my workshop in her district in Delano, California. She was having difficulties finding an address for her students to write the author. So, she e-mailed me:

> We recently finished reading *The Pigman*. However, we were also finishing *Antigone*, so the postcard assignment was postponed for almost a week (I was afraid I lost their momentum, but I was wrong). . . . the results were great . . . almost a 95 percent turn-in rate. I have almost one hundred postcards to mail. Help! I have them already to go, but I'm not quite sure if I mail to the publisher or author, and I need a template of a cover letter to send with the postcards. The kids can't believe that I am really going to mail them (so I really have to). . . .

I knew that I needed to help her, so I searched the Web for Paul Zindel, but I couldn't find any contact information. I did learn two things though: first, that Zindel had passed away a few years ago (bad news), and second, that Scholastic was his publisher (good news). I contacted my editor at Scholastic who found out that Zindel's mail is still handled by his original publisher, Harper & Row. I was able to pass along to Mary an address and contact person to try there:

Mrs. Helen Lane
Harper & Row
10 E. 53rd St.
New York, NY 10022

But what if I didn't have a contact who was so resourceful? What are we going to do if the author is no longer alive?

I have three thoughts on this.

1. **Have students write to the author anyway.** Obviously, you can't mail students' writing anywhere, but students should be able to understand the situation and still be willing to write a critical review with their audience in mind. Think of all the assignments in school that students have written to and for the teacher: We have overused ourselves as an audience for student writing, and students will be surprised with their new audience even if the author can no longer respond.

> If you can find an interview with the deceased author, have students read it. This will allow them to get to know the author a bit better. For example, I found an interview with Paul Zindel conducted by students and published on Scholastic's Authors & Book page at http://books.scholastic.com/teachers/authorsandbooks, which I recommended to Mary.

2. **Change the assignment.** Have students write to a character in the book. Again, no mailing can occur, and the format of the writing will need to be adjusted, but at least students will engage in critical analysis. See "Dear Character" letters in Chapter 1 (pages 36–38) for some ideas.

3. **Find a surrogate audience.** Even though I think options 1 and 2 above are reasonable compromises, some classes will lose the energy required for this assignment if their postcards, memos, or letters won't really be sent. Investigate whether there is a fan club, a representative, or a family member still handling the author's affairs. This is not a perfect solution, but it's worth a try.

✛✛✛✛✛✛✛✛✛✛✛✛✛✛✛✛✛✛ Reality Check ✛✛✛✛✛✛✛✛✛✛✛✛✛✛✛✛✛✛

Despite our best efforts, some authors do not write back, even when we've contacted them in advance and requested (or begged for!) a reply—even when students have poured time and energy into their work and are eagerly awaiting a response. What do we do when authors let the reader-writer circle be broken?

We can accept and even discuss with students why this might have happened. For example, you might explain that young-adult authors are very busy people. We may fantasize about the lifestyle of a rich, successful writer, but these people work very hard. (I'll bet they put in workdays as long as ours.) We must remember that authors are not sitting around their villas waiting for the daily mail to arrive.

Another consideration is that authors move on to new projects and may not be keen on comments on past work. When students read a short story, a novel, an article, a textbook chapter, or whatever else you assign them, it is new to *them*. But the piece probably was written years ago, and it most likely is not a front-burner item for the author any longer. The excitement of praising, or questioning, or suggesting polishing to an author from the students' perspective may very well be boring, a distraction, or even a puzzlement from the author's perspective. Imagine a published author feeling energized by reading 29 memos about a book he or she wrote 12 years ago. It is possible, but not for all authors. We must remember this, and we can explain this to our students.

We can also simply let it go. If the author does not write back to the class, it's all right. Not ideal, of course, but it's okay. Students will feel disappointed, but they'll get over it. In my experience they ask me each day for a week or two, "Did we get a letter back yet?", and eventually all kids, even the most persistent, will, by the third week, have forgotten about it, and we're finally off the hook.

The upside is that we know that even without an author's reply, the talk-back assignment has merit; it fosters careful, purposeful reading, and it motivates careful, purposeful writing.

This chapter was designed to fill in some gaps in the reading-writing approach I call "talking back to authors." An important piece of this approach to reading response is the actual delivery of student-to-author feedback. The examples in this chapter underscore the importance of being resourceful in searching the Internet for information that can connect students with authors. While it is not essential that students' work actually be sent to the writer, it motivates students, giving them a real purpose and the expectation that the author will engage them in a meaningful conversation.

When your students have succeeded with basic responses to an author—and, enjoyed receiving an author's feedback—you may feel that they're ready to go deeper in their responses and write in more-sophisticated formats. In the next chapter, we look at a few ideas for stretching student's critical thinking in response to fiction and nonfiction texts with more-challenging response formats.

CHAPTER 6

ADVANCED READER-RESPONSE ASSIGNMENTS

Dear Kevin,

Thank you for sharing your students' work with me. I enjoyed looking at the sample booklets you sent.

I have not heard of this type of project before, but it seems like you had good results from it. It makes me think of the old phrase "you don't really know a subject until you try to teach it." Well, you did exactly that for your students, right? You asked them to "teach" by rewriting a chapter from my book.

Thanks again for sharing this idea with me, and please tell them that I said "hello."

—Mathematics professor and textbook author

In Chapters 1 and 2 we considered a set of writing structures that support student response to both fiction and nonfiction reading assignments. We examined student-authored postcards, memos, and letters from various grade levels on various subjects. We explored ways to make the reading-writing assignments purposeful and motivating for students while teaching strategies to support careful, attentive reading and to foster analytic writing that reflects students' unique voices.

And we can take our students further. This chapter provides three additional writing structures that build upon the earlier ones and help students develop their critical-thinking skills: study guides, textbook chapter rewrites, and letters to authors for the Letters about Literature Contest. These assignments can be used to differentiate instruction when you have some students who are ready for more-advanced work or when you have used the earlier suggested assignments with the whole class and now everyone is ready to move up the talk-back ladder.

Student-Authored Study Guides

Recall from Chapter 2 the physical science chapter study guide for which ninth grader Olivia wrote a student-to-publisher Proposal Letter. The idea was to have students offer their study guides as a supplemental resource in a proposal letter written to the book's publisher (see pages 63–66). Now it is time to revisit this idea and examine the study guide reading-writing assignment in more detail.

The chapter study guide assignment requires students to evaluate the reading at a more advanced level than the postcard and memo assignments. So many complex thinking tasks occur when students write a synopsis of a textbook chapter (or an assigned article, a Web site, or any other nonfiction resource). Students who write a study guide learn the following skills:

- reading the text carefully to understand the information presented

- prioritizing important information by determining key ideas and eliminating unnecessary details

- translating the author's original words into student-friendly language

- deciding on the layout, organization, and visuals to include in the guide

- developing study and review questions

- providing teaching tips for learning the material

> English/language arts teachers can use this same assignment for a novel or play. In fact, teacher and author Jim Burke gave me the idea to have students compose a CliffNotes™-like guide for a literature assignment (2000).

The following examples show approaches for a reading-writing response in a language arts class and a physical science course.

APOSTROPHE HANDBOOK

Fifth graders in Craig Smith's class at New Hope Middle School in New Hope, Pennsylvania, wrote Apostrophe Handbooks to cement their understanding of apostrophe usage. Craig designed a simple cover page with a decorative frame and the title *Handbook of Apostrophes* and made a class set of copies. He handed these out to students along with blank pages. Students put the cover sheet on top, folded the sheets together, and stapled them along the fold to create an eight-page booklet.

In his guidelines, Craig required students to explain on the interior pages four rules for using apostrophes to form:

- plurals of letters, numbers, and signs

- contractions

- singular possessives

- plural possessives

The guidelines also required that students include an example to illustrate the rule and an explanation of any "hard-to-understand" exceptions to the rule.

One student, Nicole, decided to include cartoon-figure "tour guides" in her handbook to help the reader navigate the information. She created Amy the Apostrophe who states the rule, X the Example who provides an illustration of the rule, and Curious the Question Mark who explains special rules.

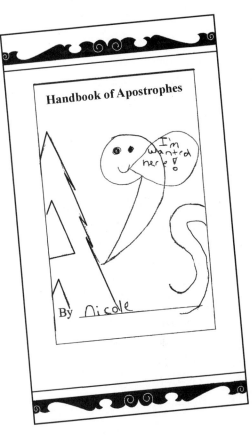

Handbook of Apostrophes

I'm wanted here!

By Nicole

Tour Guides

"Hi, I'm Amy the apostrophe and I help guide you through this book with the rules."

"Hi, I'm X the example and I help by showing you examples."

"Hi, I'm Curious the Question Mark and I help out when there is a special rule for that page."

How to form Plurals with apostrophes

"You can use 's. to form the plural of letters, numbers or signs."

"A's are my main grad

X the example wrote A's because it shows that X gets more than one A for grades."

How to use apostrophes for missing letters or numbers

"you can write an apostrophe for missing letters or numbers."

"'96 was the year I graduated in."

"X the example wrote '96 because he is missing the 19 in 1996

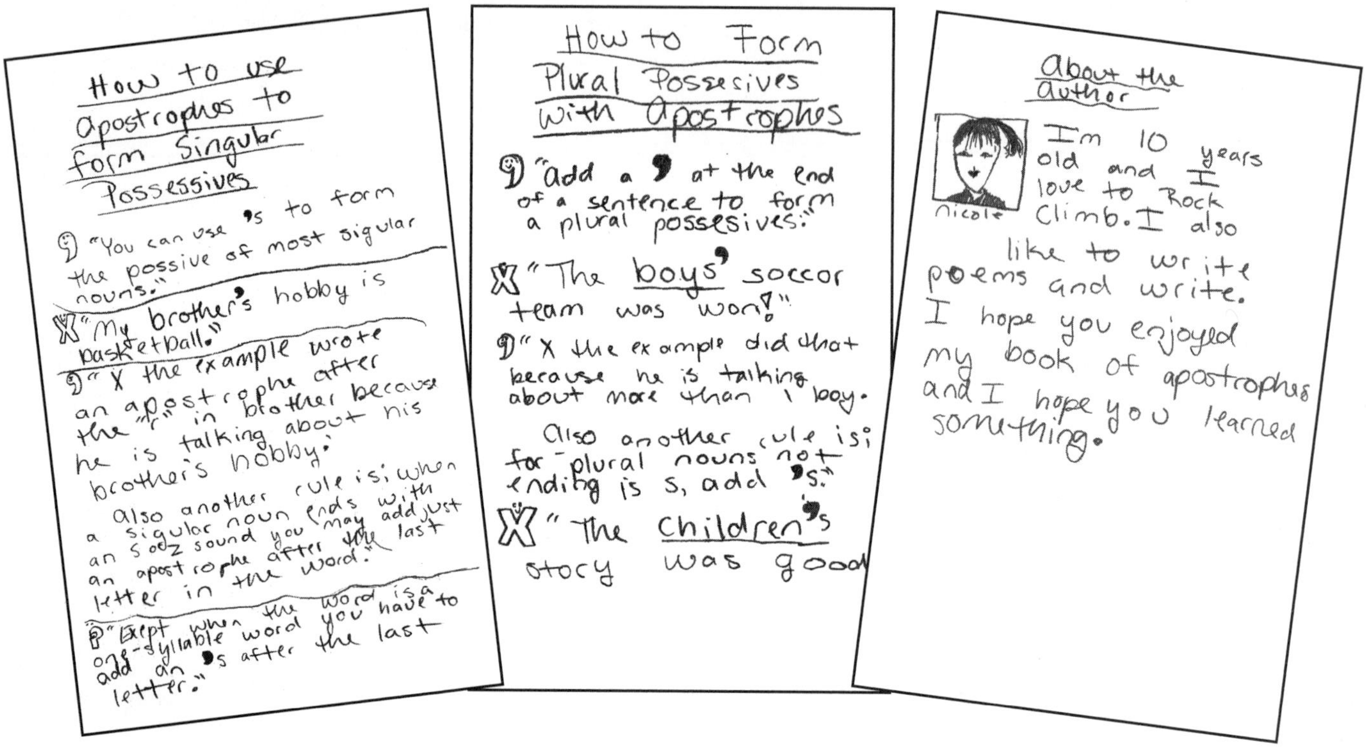

Handwritten handbook pages (student writing):

Page 1:
How to use apostrophes to form Singular Possessives

1) "You can use 's to form the possive of most sigular nouns."

✗ "My brother's hobby is basketball."

2) "✗ the example wrote an apostrophe after the "r" in brother because he is talking about his brother's hobby."

Also another rule is: when a sigular noun ends with an s or z sound you may add just an apostrophe after the last letter in the word.

3) "Exept when the word is a one-syllable word you have to add an 's after the last letter."

Page 2:
How to Form Plural Possesives with apostrophes

1) "add a 9 at the end of a sentence to form a plural possesives:"

✗ "The boys' soccer team was won?"

2) "✗ the example did that because he is talking about more than 1 boy.

Also another rule is: for plural nouns not ending is s, add 's."

✗ "the children's story was good

Page 3:
about the author

I'm 10 years old and I love to Rock Climb. I also like to write poems and write. I hope you enjoyed my book of apostrophes and I hope you learned something.

nicole

Smith has the students refer to their own handbook rather than the grammar textbook when they encounter a question on apostrophes in their writing. However, he finds that they do not need to use this resource very often because the act of composing the handbook really taught them the rules they needed to learn. He comments, "Before we had these handbooks, my students were floundering. We didn't know a plural possessive from a singular noun."

When your students create a study guide, you might choose to have them write a cover letter to the publisher offering them as resources for the company to consider adding to their publications (see page 116). While it's a long shot, this approach usually motivates students to revise and polish diligently: They anticipate that their writing may reach a potentially huge audience. Or, the study guide booklets may remain in the classroom as in-house learning resources for the student-writer, his or her peers, and next semester's or year's class. A smaller, more local audience, to be sure, but still a viable option.

PHYSICAL SCIENCE CHAPTER REVIEW BOOKLET

Older students, too, enjoy this reading-writing activity. You've already had a first peek at Olivia's "Chapter 3 Study Guide" for her Physical Science textbook in Chapter 2. The purpose of the assignment was to get students more engaged with the reading and learning of the science concepts on Newton's Laws of Motion.

Teacher Jud Landis required that students write a synopsis of the chapter's nine sections. He provided a template with the chapter's subheadings to help them organize their booklets. Olivia included all of the required elements: formulas, illustrations, and a glossary of key vocabulary used in the chapter.

Section 3.1
Galileo Developed the Concept of Acceleration

6

- Galileo defined the rate of change of velocity as acceleration

acceleration - any change in motion

- $a = \Delta v / t$ accel. = change in velocity / time interval

- changes in acceleration include: slowing down, speeding up, change in direction, or change in speed & direction
- (slowing down is called deceleration or negative acceleration)

Δ = Greek letter delta. means "change in"

EXAMPLE = Bike increases speed from 10 m/s → 20 m/s in 5 sec. What was the acc.

acceleration on earth = 10 m/s²

$a = \Delta v/t$ = final speed - original speed / time
= 20 m/s - 10 m/s / 5 sec = 10 m/s / 5 sec = 2 m/s / sec = 2 m/s²

- Free fall acceleration is caused gravity

- the acceleration due to gravity on earth is 10 m/s²

EXAMPLE = If you drop a penny off a bridge, will it accelerate

2

Yes

Section 3.1
Continued

Galileo discovered that when he rolled a ball down an incline, the ball gains the same amount of velocity in equal time intervals.

→ (In other words, their speed increased by a given amount in each second)

A body undergoes acceleration when there is a **change** in its state of motion.

3

Section 3.6
Friction Is a Force That Affects Motion

6

- friction always acts in a direction to oppose motion

Friction or when one object rubs against something else

friction occurs for solids, liquids, & gases

EXAMPLE = If you drag a solid block along a floor to the left, the force of friction on the block will be to the right.

- air drag - the force of friction that acts on an object when it falls through the air

- amount of friction depends on what what is being pressed against what

Applied force just overcomes friction so the crate slides at a constant velocity... so $\Sigma F = 0$

9

Section 3.7
Objects in Free Fall Have Equal Acceleration

- free fall - falling only under the influence of gravity, where other forces such as air drag can be neglected

- the greater the slope of the incline, the greater the acceleration of the ball. When incline is vertical, acceleration is that of free fall

- acceleration doesn't depend on mass & neither does free fall

EXAMPLE = A 10-kg boulder & 1-kg stone dropped from an elevated position at the same time will fall together & strike the ground at practically the same time.

10

good detail point

In addition to setting clear guidelines, Jud gave his students a purpose that inspired them to turn in excellent products. When they had almost completed a draft, he told them, "You have done a very solid job learning about Newton's Laws of Motion. I am a bit concerned, however, that my next class may have more difficulty with it, so may I have your permission to make copies of your booklets to share with them next semester?" The draft quality went up; these students wanted to look good in front of their peers. They may not have admitted this, but I believe it's true. Students are proud to take on the role of co-teacher.

Olivia sought to expand her audience further by submitting her guide with a proposal letter to the author, which got an encouraging response, but not an acceptance (see page 65), and then sent a similar proposal letter to the publisher. As of the printing of this book, we are still waiting for a response—and if it never arrives, that's okay, too. Olivia and her classmates have already benefited from the assignment: reading, writing, and thinking about science.

MATH TERM STUDY GUIDE

You can also offer a simpler format for a more focused study. John Waldron, a fifth-grade teacher at Paul W. Kutz School in Doylestown, Pennsylvania, assigned students to author their own Math Terms booklet to help them learn and remember key terms in the math textbook. John identified 42 important state-mandated terms but felt that this would be too many for each student to write about, so he divided the list into sets of eight or nine terms and randomly assigned students to work with a set. He required his students

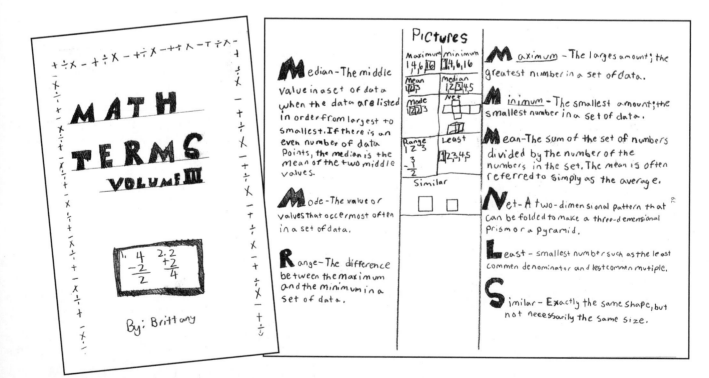

to illustrate each definition to demonstrate their understanding of word meanings. Page 112 shows an example from Brittany's illustrated Math Terms book in which she defines and draws a picture to describe each term in the M–S set. Not only did she have fun writing her booklet, she was cementing her understanding of the required content.

If you assign different parts or sections of the reading material to students, as John did with the math terms, ask students to pair up with peers who have been assigned different terms, and have the partners discuss and trade their booklets. This JigSaw-activity format allows you to break a large chunk of content information into manageable pieces that students can learn and teach one another.

TIPS FOR HELPING STUDENTS CREATE QUALITY STUDY GUIDES

While student-written study guides can be powerful and motivating projects, most students need support to help them create quality guides like Nicole's and Olivia's. To increase the likelihood of success for all students on this assignment, I suggest that we recognize that the quality of student output is directly related to the quality of teaching input. Here are some ways to ensure that everyone moves forward:

1. Provide students with a scoring device, like a ChecBric, early in the assignment, which delineates the requirements and the point values. Have students use it to set goals for their work before writing and evaluate their progress during and after they've written the guide.

2. Share examples of past student responses (both successful and in need of improvement), and have students identify the strengths and weaknesses of the writing.

3. Show students a CliffsNotes™ guide, and ask whether they know what purpose it serves readers. This is a good way to introduce the concept of a synopsis as well as present authentic, published writing in this format.

4. Reveal to students the potential pitfalls of the task, such as merely copying word-for-word phrases from the text, hitting some key concepts while missing others, and sloppy writing, which interferes with the potential usefulness of the guide.

✛✛✛✛✛✛✛✛✛✛✛✛✛✛ Reality Check ✛✛✛✛✛✛✛✛✛✛✛✛✛✛

Even with lots of scaffolding, we no doubt will find that some students still struggle with this task. That's okay. The attempt, the pursuit of taking existing information from an expert and working to present it in a simpler form, is valuable in itself. The process of summarizing, paraphrasing, and developing a synopsis is even more valuable than the finished product.

5. Encourage experimentation and variation with the assignment. Tell students that they may find creative ways to explain the concepts they summarize, including the use of cartoon figures to narrate, the addition of practice test questions (with answers provided elsewhere in the guide), or the invention of a new format or layout that is different, and potentially better than, the text's.

If you choose to give students an opportunity later in the term or year to write another study guide on a new topic, then you can expect improvement with this rigorous reading-writing assignment. You may want to add a degree of challenge by adding one or more criteria to the assignment, such as *include study review questions.*

Textbook Chapter Rewrites

When asked about the effectiveness of his pre-algebra textbook, seventh grader Robby told me, "My math book is like a tranquilizer; it puts me to sleep." The book received similar reviews from other students. That's one reason Robby's teacher Kevin Callahan decided to have the class rewrite the last chapter of the book. Kevin also wanted students to absorb as much as they could about linear equations and graphs, the subject of the chapter. Their understanding of the material would serve as an entrée to algebra next year.

To set up this brand-new assignment, Kevin and I developed the following procedure:

1. **Form groups of three.** Kevin knew his kids quite well by the end of the year, so each group had three expert roles: a good mathematician, a good illustrator, and a good writer. Each group was then assigned a different section of the chapter.

2. **Provide clear expectations.** We designed a ChecBric for students that clearly outlined the parameters of this assignment (pages 90–91).

3. **State and restate (and restate again) the purposes of the assignment.** We planned to reiterate the three main goals throughout the project:

   - to improve the textbook so that you will understand and remember the important math concepts in the chapter

   - to assist Mr. Callahan with teaching next year's class

   - to show the textbook company some ideas for possible improvement

4. **Photocopy the chapter's seven sections.** Each group received a different section of the chapter to "mark up." We explained how to delete boring parts; add better examples; insert clear, more descriptive words; and move text around to reorganize the information.

5. Establish ground rules. Ours included:

- All three team members must contribute.

- Decisions should be by consensus, but if not, the decision goes to the role expert.

- Volume of voices should not distract other groups.

- Groups must meet daily completion targets.

Here is the result of this challenging task from the group of math students who were assigned to rewrite Section 11.2 , Scatter Plots. Kevin was especially impressed by the example they developed on page 3—the students' example relates algebraic principles to solving a problem that would capture the interest of other preteens: estimating concessions earnings at a football game.

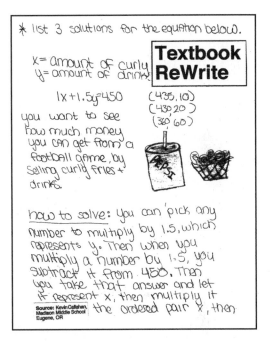

ANTICIPATING THE RESULTS

I get very excited when I am in a classroom of students who are busy rewriting an assigned textbook chapter. The very idea of students going beyond a critical analysis to attempting to *improve* a given resource makes teaching a wondrous thing. You know that I am an advocate of student-authored study guides and chapter review booklets. But this assignment is even more challenging because it elevates students to Bloom's synthesis level: "Creatively or divergently applying prior knowledge and skills to produce a new or original whole."

More in-depth than a summary, a rewrite requires taking the given, deciding what's valuable to keep, deciding what is missing or needed, merging the new into the old, reformatting it, and producing a new expression of the content information in an engaging product. Whew. Lots of work. But Benjamin Bloom would be proud to see students working at this advanced level of thinking.

Expecting great results with this demanding task—even with scaffolding—may be overly optimistic. As his seventh and eighth graders worked ambitiously on rewriting their sections, I expressed cautious optimism about the final products. Kevin reassured me, "I am already pleased. The process they're going through is making them better math students."

He's right: In order to even attempt to rewrite a section of the math book, the students are approaching mathematics differently. The assignment makes them change their stance from passive student to active cowriter. When you work with students on a chapter rewrite, keep in mind the principle "process over product," though we are working with students to be successful in both areas.

TIPS FOR HELPING STUDENTS REWRITE TEXTBOOK CHAPTERS

Rewriting a chapter is a brand-new venture for students, and they certainly won't have any idea on how to proceed. In fact, they usually don't even believe you are assigning them this task in all seriousness. Here are some ideas to help you set up this assignment properly so that students won't panic—or revolt.

1. **Show them sample study guides.** Let students see what a study guide is, why they are written, and what their limitations are. If your students have not written study guides before, show them a published study guide, such as CliffsNotes™ as an example. These guides provide great summaries, but they don't attempt at improving the original. Tell your students that they are going to do better than Cliff—or any other study guide.

2. **Explain the difference between summarizing and synthesizing.** Study guides, chapter-review booklets, and CliffsNotes summarize important information and try to package that information into a user-friendly, easily understandable format. Rewrites, on the other hand, require synthesizing: taking the existing version, making decisions about what is successful or unsuccessful, and then merging what works into a newly written version—much harder.

3. **Divide the chapter into manageable sections and assign each section to a small group or pairs to rewrite.** Provide enough time for partners or groups to collaborate on the revision—I usually allow three or four periods (roughly three hours).

4. **Provide them with a road map.** I recommend creating a ChecBric for this assignment that details the assignment criteria and your expectations (see Chapter 4). I've found that students use both the checklist section and the rubric to evaluate their progress. You are welcome to adapt the ChecBric Kevin and I designed for your rewrite assignments (pages 90–91).

Next Step: A Proposal Letter to the Textbook Publishing Company

To reinforce the connection between students and authors, you may want to consider getting the students to write a letter to the textbook publisher proposing that their study guide booklets or improved chapter rewrites be considered for publication as a supplemental resource to the textbook—an assignment I described in Chapter 2. The act of proposing to have their work published moves students along the road into the Club of Readers and Writers.

In addition to the letter writing tips and suggestions I made in Chapter 2, here are some reminders to help you make the most of the assignment:

1. **Clearly and honestly reveal to students the difficulty of being published.** Students should understand that acceptance of any writing by a publisher is a long shot. Tell them lots of good ideas go unpublished; it's a shame, but there are limitations that all publishers face.

2. **Contact the publisher in advance.** Just as I recommended contacting authors in advance of sending student postcards, memos, and friendly letters, I suggest that the teacher do some "downfield blocking" for student-writers on this proposal letter. In your letter or e-mail, inform the publisher that you have purchased and use their textbook, and explain the context of the study guide assignment. Let them know that the students' proposals are coming, and that they understand the tough decisions publishers must make but are looking forward to a response. Such an effort can only increase the likelihood that you and your students will receive a reply.

3. **Gain the support of the lead author.** Before sending a letter to the publisher, you may want to have students contact the textbook's lead author about this proposal to win over a potential, powerful ally who could advocate on their behalf to the publisher. Of course, this requires students to write and revise another letter, and it requires you to help edit the letter, reproduce another copy of the booklets, and send out more mail. Instead, you may want to write the letter on their behalf, the way Kevin Callahan did for his math students who rewrote the final chapter in their textbook. (See his letter on page 103.)

The author took the time to reply, and his letter is presented at the beginning of this chapter (page 107). His response reveals the tremendous potential this "talk-back" assignment has. For a university professor and textbook author to salute and celebrate students' work is very important. And while he did not offer to advocate them to his publisher, his endorsement of the assignment proves the benefit.

Letters About Literature (Fiction and Nonfiction)

Here's a third advanced reading-writing structure that you may assign for any content area: Students write a personal letter to an author whose work has had a profound affect on them and submit it to the Letters About Literature Contest. The contest Web site invites readers in grades 4 through 12 to participate in a national reading-writing contest. To enter, "readers write a personal letter to an author, living or dead, from any genre—fiction or nonfiction, contemporary or classic—explaining how that author's work changed the student's way of thinking about the world or themselves."

The contest advocates writing in response to literature as a way to build comprehension and connect reading and writing for academic and personal growth. The Web site states:

> Research has shown that children gain greater understanding of what they have read when they are given frequent opportunities to respond to what they've read, especially through writing. The writing response, in turn, helps to develop the students' critical reading and thinking skills. And so the cycle goes—children who read, write better; children who write, read more. This reading-writing link is the very heart of the Letters About Literature (LAL) program (2006).

That is precisely the message of this book. If this contest looks interesting to you, consider several approaches.

1. **Assign the whole class to enter.** You may want to have each student write about a book of their choice or all students write about a class favorite.

2. **Assign a reading group to enter, with each student composing a letter about his or her favorite book.** This would be a good way to pilot the assignment one year to see how it goes. (I wouldn't automatically select the most advanced group.)

3. **Make it optional.** Put the contest out to students, talk it up, and see who is interested. You may want to offer some extra-credit points to get their attention.

4. **E-mail the LAL Project Director** at lettersaboutlit@epix.net to receive a 24-page educational supplement resource with lessons, activities, and reproducible pages to assist you in guiding students through the book discussion and writing process.

The Contest Web site lists the winning student letter writers by state. In my state of Oregon, sixth grader Latricia from Oaklea Middle School in Junction City was honored for winning a statewide writing contest, and she is also one of six students, out of 45,000, to win the national Letters About Literature Contest. She was flown to Washington, D.C., for the National Book Festival and to receive her award from the Librarian of Congress. Her letter appears on page 119.

This is very powerful writing on a very personal topic. Latricia not only connected the book to her own experiences, she used the book to gain a new perspective on those experiences. And as she thanks the author for the insights she has gained, she speaks to him as a real person—she communicates with the creator of the book. Her conclusion thanking Pelzer for inspiring her and helping shape her "perspective on life" connects the reader-writer circle.

12/1/04

Dear Mr. David Pelzer,

One year ago, I read your book, *The Child Called It*. I am an 11-year-old foster child living in Junction City, Oregon. I remember the day my foster mom, Cheryl, gave me your book. She told me that she wanted me to take a look at this book because I was always complaining how hopeless and grim I thought my life was.

When I moved to my foster home on August 10, 2001, I thought my life was going to continue being sad and unpredictable. When I lived with my biological parents, I didn't know whether I'd have to call the paramedics for my abused mom OR whether I'd have to save myself from my abusive step-dad. My step-dad would slap me across the face, and I'd go flying across the room. I was living in fear of him. Every day I would have a new bruise or scratch on me. Sometimes my teachers would get suspicious and start asking questions, but I always covered up what was happening to me at home; I didn't want to be taken away because I was scared that he would come after me. My step-dad told me that I was worthless and stupid and that I wound never amount to anything. He said that I'd end up just like my mother. I believed him after a while.

Even though I moved to a new home, at first, I still felt like I was out of place with my foster family. I continued to feel totally alone in the world. My foster mom gave me *The Child Called It* to read after I had moved in. I had no idea what the book was going to be about. I predicted that it was just going to be about a little boy who was bullied at school and called "IT." As I got into your book, I soon realized that this book was going to be a book that would change my life. As I was about halfway through your book, especially the part about your mom treating you like a speck of dirt, I realized that I was lucky to have Cheryl and John (my foster parents) in my life. My perspective on life was changing as I read your words. Suddenly, I realized that I now had more love and support than other children and that I needed to treasure what I currently had and not focus on the painful times of my past. It felt like each sentence of yours was searing into my heart and triggering something inside of me that I had never felt. It's hard to explain what I was feeling when I read certain passages of your story. I felt like the images you were creating for me paralyzed me for a nanosecond; it shocked me that someone could survive the abuse you described. Toward the end of your book, I felt like the hopelessness and distress I was feeling was falling away.

Slowly, as the hopelessness and distress went away, I had more room to open up and listen to my foster parents. They told me the truth about my biological family. I had been lied to all my life, even my biological mom, whom I had trusted and protected, had been deceiving me.

After I read your book, I knew that none of the abuse was my fault. You showed me that I had a voice that I never knew I had. It was the voice of my thoughts. Your story continues to help me today when I feel irritated and a bit down on myself. I know that people can be what they want to be and achieve what they want to if they are determined. Mr. Pelzer, you have inspired me to try my best to be what I want to be. I am going to have the best life I can. You have truly helped me with my perspective on life. For this, I thank you!

Love,

Latricia

Challenging Authority Through Advanced Talk-Back Assignments:

In Chapter 1, I cited Alfie Kohn's call for fostering "challenging students"—young people who learn how to challenge "the very idea of authority" in school. He advocates:

> Avoiding practices that encourage passivity is just the beginning, of course. Teachers also must take steps to create critical classrooms and to set up regular opportunities for students to be skeptical about what they hear. The choice of reading matter plays a role here. When a teacher deliberately assigns material that contains errors or clear indications of the author's point of view, students can be jolted into the recognition that something in print shouldn't be accepted at face value. The teacher can help students develop the disposition and the skills necessary to notice mistakes and biases even in works where these things may not be so close to the surface (2004).

Kohn is urging us to help students "talk back" to author(ity): We can teach them to critique the accuracy of the content they read; to analyze content that is privileged or ignored; and to determine whether the author clearly states his or her point of view and purpose for writing or masks it. Specifically, Kohn wants us to help students develop an awareness that "authors are fallible and have distinctive points of view." This means teaching students to read with a focus on the person behind the words so that they hold the author responsible for his or her words. Kohn believes that if students develop a "questioning stance" toward the assigned reading, we can avoid teaching "the hidden curriculum": lessons that cultivate passivity, encourage students to please authority, and congratulate students when they mindlessly accept everything they read or hear.

In fact, we can angle our reading-response assignments to help students change their stance from passive to active, and beyond that—to challenging—using Kohn's ideas. We can assign postcards, memos, letters, study guides, or chapter rewrites that aim to redefine the student-authority relationship.

To succeed with this more advanced type of critique, students need to draw upon the usual talk-back tools, such as a polite and respectful tone and strategies for praising, asking questions, and making suggestions for polishing. They must also do the following:

- possess a high degree of content expertise

- know about alternative points of view on a topic

- know about new research available

- use supplemental resources

- know how to distinguish between facts and opinions

• know how to identify missing information

That is, they must know what they are talking about.

This means, of course, that we need to do the following:

- allocate time and provide resources for students to delve into the topic that is presented in the reading they will respond to

- teach research skills so they can follow hunches and lines of thinking

- review compare-and-contrast skills so students can determine the way and the extent to which different sources cover a topic

> For outstanding resources on teaching students to take an inquisitive, questioning stance, visit the Rethinking Schools Web site at http://www.rethinkingschools.org.

- model careful note-taking skills so they can record the information as they go

- review how to identify fact and opinion in writing

- practice identifying an author's point of view, the author's purpose, and the author's intent

Here are two response assignments in which students took a questioning stance.

The first one comes from my eighth-grade U.S. History/Language Arts Block class at James Monroe Middle School in Eugene, Oregon. It was early in the course, and we were studying the history of European exploration. The course textbook included a short description of Columbus's first settlement in the Americas, Fort La Navidad. The students read the passage to learn what happened to the Fort while Columbus and most of the crew had returned to Spain to report to the monarchs on his first voyage.

To: Ernest R. M.
From: Tana
Date: September 30, 1997
Re: "Christmas Day, 1492"

I think the story "Christmas Day, 1492" is well-written. I liked the part about it being God's will that the ship sank. It is short, but you didn't leave out a lot of detail. You could have added what, exactly, happened to Fort La Navidad. I want to know who burned it and killed the men, and I want to know why they did it.

Tana is beginning to develop her questioning stance. First, she starts with the positive—what worked for her as a history student. Then she politely, but directly, informs the textbook's lead author what did not work, and she lets him know what key information is missing. This is just a start in becoming a "challenging" student, but a start is a positive thing.

The second talk-back assignment came later in the course, in the unit on Colonial America. In this student-to-author feedback, the student-writer demonstrates a deeper, more developed critical stance. The task is the same as the 1492 memo: Critique the

Dear Ernest R. M. and coauthors,

I am an eighth grader from Monroe Middle School writing in regards to the passage in the book A Proud Nation on page 143, "Hunting for Witches." My class and I studied the Salem witch trials for quite some time. We have used many sources including your textbook in order to gather all the information that we needed. Now I am writing to tell you my evaluation on how well you described the situation.

First of all, I must say you have included very accurate information, dates, and definitions. This was an enjoyable article that told about one woman's trial and how unfair it was. The picture added to the detail and reality of the tragic event.

Still, I do have some constructive criticism and suggestions for your well-written article. You only explained about one person and their opinion without explaining what went on in the trial. Take for instance the girls' afflictions and convulsions that caused the magistrate to charge people and punish them. If you're going to do writing with illustrations and photographs, you should have them match. The illustration you had inserted showed the trial of a man while you talked of a woman's trial.

My class and I wished to see from what source you obtained the illustration. Upon looking at the credits, we found them to be listed by the source when it would have been much easier to search for the page number. I took the liberty of searching for the page of the picture and did not succeed in finding the credit for page 143.

I also have a question for you: Why didn't you add any theories as to how the hysteria of the witch trials started? That would have made it more interesting.

Overall, I feel that the information given was not enough for eighth graders because we learned much more looking upon other sources.

Sincerely,

Courtney

December 1, 1997

book's information, and address the text's lead author. But the topic is different: Salem witch trials, and so is the format: a longer letter instead of a memo.

Courtney is accomplishing much here, both in content and structure. In her introduction she wisely sets the context for her audience, and she provides him with her topic sentence. Her first body paragraph congratulates the author for what he did well. (I had urged the students to begin with the positive). Her next two body paragraphs include her "constructive criticism" of the chapter. She also supports her opinions with precise examples from the text, so that her audience will get her point. Her fourth body paragraph poses a question that leads to another critique about the incomplete treatment of the topic. Finally, her conclusion paragraph nicely summarizes her position. And throughout her letter she uses respectful words and a polite tone. Courtney is swimming with the big fish, and now that she's done it, she has permanently changed her relationship with authors. A transformative experience.

In both these examples, students go beyond a basic critique to a meatier analysis. It is what Edward H. Behrman describes as reading from a "resistant perspective" (2006). These students are beginning to read and interpret a social studies textbook from a position far more critical, more questioning, more suspicious of authority than that of the traditional, passive consumer who reads to regurgitate. Further steps in this direction would be to attempt to identify the author's point of view toward these historical events and to scrutinize his or her intent—mere information sharing or a subtle passing on a particular attitude or position on the information.

I realize that introducing such an assignment may feel a little sticky at first: It's one thing to have your students write to an author suggesting a plot change in a short story or adding more illustrations to a math text; it's quite another when students write to an author to point out negligent coverage or a one-sided perspective. This drifts into a more political or social analysis and critique.

Yet, it is our job to teach students to think while also teaching them the content. Critical thinking is not just for the classroom. In fact, isn't critical thinking in school a training exercise for adulthood? Isn't everything we do in school practicing and fine-tuning skills for life? It is, and therefore we need to become comfortable with students digging into critical analysis of where an author is coming from and where she/he is heading.

Students can take a "questioning stance" when three conditions are met:

1. **Students have sufficient content knowledge.** We must be convinced that they know what they're talking about before we will consider mailing their challenges to an author. This can be accomplished by testing them for content understanding, interviewing them for knowledge on the basic facts, or grouping them for discussion of the

important ideas under study. We can require students to "pass through a gate" as a prerequisite to writing and sending challenging feedback to an author.

2. **Students use a proper tone of voice.** They must prove that they realize the audience of their feedback, the author, is a person, a real human being with real human emotions. So the tone of the letter, memo, whatever structure is used, must be polite and respectful—without scolding or huffiness. This is required for all feedback communications, but it is especially important here. Polite and respectful discourse is something our country could use more of.

3. **Students are inquiring, not accusing.** They must understand that the purpose of this reading-writing assignment is to initiate a dialogue with the author about the content and to continue to learn about it with the author. The purpose is not a monologue, an angry diatribe, an isolating experience. A dialogue can be accomplished by instructing students to use a question-asking approach rather than a statement-making approach. By framing their concerns in the form of questions, they can avoid the trap of accusing or condemning the author for the decisions made in the writing. Questions allow students to raise areas of concern without triggering a defensive reaction from an author who may feel puzzled, annoyed, or frustrated by a perceived hostility from students.

We made a leap in this last chapter. We examined three advanced writing structures that build upon ones we addressed in the first two chapters to elevate our students' critical reading and writing. All of these assignments provide elements of surprise and challenge that motivate students to engage fully in responding to textbooks or literature: study guides that assist instruction with a helpful synopsis of textbook material, textbook chapter rewrites that require students to use higher-order thinking skills to edit and improve upon the author's work, and personal letters in which a student explains to an author how his or her work has positively affected the student's life—the reading-writing connection we want them to make.

Finally, we set some goals for designing assignments to cultivate critical learners who challenge authority to learn—students who know how to effectively and responsibly talk back.

As you approach these advanced reader-response assignments, keep in mind that they are demanding; they show students your high expectations of them and your belief in their abilities to soar. At the same time, they must also be doable. Scaffolding students' work with guidelines, models, discussion about your expectations, and opportunities to revise—as demonstrated throughout this book—will help them succeed.

CONCLUSION

I became a teacher 32 years ago, in 1974, because I believed that school should be a place of inquiry and that students should be inquisitive. My job as the teacher was to provide opportunities and structures for their inquiry.

I believed back then that real learning is based on wanting to know something. I still do.

The problem is, teaching and learning in school very easily devolves into the teacher telling the students about the subject and then the students parroting back to the teacher what they've heard or read. It's a cycle that's predictable and not very exciting for them—or us.

Talking back to authors is exciting because it is inquiry-based. Students read what we assign with the purpose of questioning the author, inquiring about the choices the author made in composing the text, querying the author in order to establish a dialogue.

This approach to reading—this stance—is very different for students. It changes the equation mightily. Students are transformed into players, participants, and partakers in the literacy exchange. They become bona fide members of the Club of Readers and Writers. Right where they belong. And that makes our teaching, and their learning, exciting.

Talk Back to the Author!

Keep the reader-writer communication alive by sending me your feedback—I'd love to hear from you. I invite you to send any adapted or modified assignments, any new ChecBrics you've designed, and especially any student sample work. I may be able to share them with other teachers in my workshops and give you and your students a larger audience for their "talk backs." Contact me at larry@larrylewin.com.

References

Beattie, D. K. (1997). *Assessment in art education.* Worcester, MA: Davis Publications.

Behrman, E. H. (2006). "Teaching about language, power, and text: A review of classroom practices that support critical literacy." *Journal of Adolescent & Adult Literacy*, International Reading Association, vol. 49, no. 6, March, 2006.

Beck, I., McKeown, M., Hamilton, R. L., & Kucan, L. (1997). *Questioning the author.* Newark, DE: International Reading Association.

Burke, J. (2000). *Reading reminders.* Portsmouth, NH: Heinemann.

Cahill, B., & Hrebic, H. Stack the Deck Writing Program (http://www.stackthedeck.com/tips-great.html)

Christensen, L. (2000). *Reading, writing, and rising up: Teaching about social justice and the power of the written word.* Milwaukee, WI: Rethinking Schools.

Cohen, E. G. (1994). *Designing group work: Strategies for the heterogeneous classroom* (2nd ed.). New York: Teachers College Press.

Daniels, H. (2001). *Literature circles: Voice and choice in book clubs and reading groups.* Portland, ME: Stenhouse.

Heacox, D. (2002). *Differentiating instruction in the regular classroom.* Minneapolis, MN: Free Spirit Publishing.

Hillocks, G. as cited in *Responding to Student Writing* by Cal State Los Angeles University Writing Center (available: http://www.calstatela.edu/centers/write_cn/writresp.htm)

Kohn, A. (2004). Challenging students . . . and how to have more of them. *Phi Delta Kappan.* 11. (available: http://www.alfiekohn.org/teaching/challenging.htm)

Lewin, L. (2003). *Paving the way in reading and writing: Strategies and activities to support struggling students in grades 6–12.* San Francisco, CA: Jossey Bass.

Lewin, L. http://www.larrylewin.com

Lewin, L., & Shoemaker, B. (1998). *Great performances: Creating classroom-based assessment tasks*. Alexandria, VA: ASCD.

National Council of Teachers of English. (1980). *How to help your child become a better writer*. (available: http://www.ncte.org/about/over/positions/category/write/107687.htm)

Poetry 180. Library of Congress. (available: http://www.loc.gov/poetry/180)

Shalaway, L. (2005). *Learning to teach.*, 3rd edition. New York: Scholastic.

Soto, G. (1993). *Local news*. San Diego: Harcourt Brace Jovanovich.

Teacher Tips for Successful Parent-Teacher Conferences, (available: http://teacher.scholastic.com/products/instructor/parentconf_responses.htm)

Tomlinson, C. A. (2003). ASCD Conference on Differentiated Instruction. Chicago, IL.

Vandergrift, K. (2006). Reader Response Criticism and Resources (available: http://www.scils.rutgers.edu/~kvander/readerresponse.html)

Wilhelm, J. (2004). *Reading is seeing*. New York: Scholastic.

Wormeli, R. (2006). *Fair isn't always equal*. Portland, ME: Stenhouse.

Zindel, P. (1968). *The Pigman*. New York: Harper & Row.

Index